PRAISE FOR *ACCELERATED HEALING*

Author John Proodian does what the best teachers do—instruct from their personal experience. He weaves together testimony, insights from God's word, and well-timed humor, to walk us through his personal growth as a minister of healing. By sharing his own story—the good, the bad, and the ugly—John offers readers a priceless gift. Like a true father, he invites us to stand on his shoulders, to learn from his mistakes, and to take part in his victories. Each revelation in *Accelerated Healing* has been fought for, but is offered freely. They will ignite a hunger for all that is possible. Read this book as a gift from God. In doing so, I believe you'll become encouraged, equipped, and inspired.

—Bill Johnson
Bethel Church, Redding, CA
Author of *God Is Good*

"John Proodian's *Accelerated Healing* is an engaging read. I believe it will be a great resource to the Body of Christ to further increase understanding of the healing ministry. This book is full of many remarkable testimonies of God's miraculous power, and is written in a way that is conversational and easy to understand. John is a former student of my school and has faithfully served Dr. James Maloney for several years as his personal assistant. He carries not only an anointing for healing, but a passion for teaching others to operate in healing as well. I am excited about this book and believe it will build your faith as you read the stories of miracles and absorb the revelation that is shared."

—Randy Clark , DMin.
Founder, Global Awakening

We are living in a new day. It is no longer about the man of God, but the God of man. As such, Jesus is releasing healers throughout the earth so that His Church displays a victorious expression of power. John Proodian's book, *Accelerating Healing*, is a valuable resource for this day and hour. I personally know John, I know his values, and I relate with his own personal story. John's Christ-centric approach restores the simplicity of the Gospel—his focus is not just on principles, but rather the Prince: Jesus Christ. For too long, the church has justified powerlessness by bringing the Word of God down to the level of her experience. What I value most about John is his refusal to do this. Instead, John's message will help pull your experience up to the fullness of the Word of God, so Jesus gets His full reward.

—Chris Gore
Author of *Walking in Supernatural Healing Power*

I've known John and Janet for years and walked through life with them and would like to personally attest to the truthfulness of their testimony. I was there as John's Dad suffered, as Janet battled knee problems and I was there the day they drew a line in the sand and said no more, enough is enough. This book is a testimony of how two ordinary Christian people decided that they were going all in on Him, His love, and His gifts to broken humanity. This book is a road map for you and me to follow. So "*take it fast*" as you read this book. Be ready to receive healing and be ready to look for the opportunities that the Holy Spirit will bring across your path to minister healing to others.

—Brian Fraley

Executive Director of *Our Father's Project* ministries

John is one of the most significant healing ministers that I've sat under. He moves in humility and power. I've been in his healing meetings where people have come out of wheelchairs, tumors have dissolved, scars have disappeared, and much more. Every time John comes to minister, we see significant miracles. John's book, *Accelerated Healing*, is one of the best books on healing you will read. If you are looking to either move in the healing gift or needing healing in your body, this book will help you.

—Paul Martini

Global Awakening

Director of Events & Associate Evangelist

My Friend Dr. John Proodian has written a must-read for those wanting to minister in a lifestyle of healing. *Accelerated Healing* is a God-inspired book used to break the strongholds of unbelief and equip the saints for the ministry of healing. John's personal journey of perseverance in the ministry of healing reveals his humble heart and love for people. I can feel the pleasure and backing of God as I read *Accelerated Healing*. I'm excited for you to not only read this book, but accelerate in representing Jesus to a world that needs healing.

—Richie Seltzer

Missionary Evangelist, YWAM

Founding Pastor of Imagine Church in Calgary, Alberta

Cofounder of Burning Ones, School of Fire

In every generation, God restores truth by causing the revelation of His Word to meet the manifestation of His power. In those instances, the Church gains momentum and the fame of Jesus is magnified and His dominion is clearly seen. John Proodian is called by God to remind the world that "with God all things are possible to him that believes." *Accelerated Healing* will strengthen your faith, ignite your expectancy, dismiss your doubts, release you from religion and stir you to walk like Jesus in the earth. I highly recommend!

—Michael A. Dalton
YES Ministries International

ACCELERATED HEALING

ACCESSING JESUS' FINISHED WORK OF DIVINE HEALING

JOHN DAVID PROODIAN

DESTINY IMAGE® PUBLISHERS, INC.
P.O. Box 310, Shippensburg, PA 17257-0310
"Promoting Inspired Lives."

This book and all other Destiny Image and Destiny Image Fiction books are available at Christian bookstores and distributors worldwide.

Cover design by Eileen Rockwell
Interior design by Terry Clifton

For more information on foreign distributors, call 717-532-3040.
Reach us on the Internet: www.destinyimage.com.

ISBN 13 TP: 978-0-7684-1904-7
ISBN 13 eBook: 978-0-7684-1905-4
ISBN 13 HC: 978-0-7684-1907-8
ISBN 13 LP: 978-0-7684-1906-1

For Worldwide Distribution, Printed in the U.S.A.
2 3 4 5 6 7 8 / 22 21 20 19 18

DEDICATION

To my wife, Janet Proodian, a gift of God and the love of my heart. In the secret place, you seek the Lord early in the morning and are filled with His presence. You go about your day filled with His love, imparting Him to me and our children. You are faithful, unwavering, and unshakable. It is hard for me to grasp just how fortunate I am to be married to you!

ACKNOWLEDGMENTS

I want to thank my parents, Edward and Marilyn, who have always loved and supported me and believed there was a call of God on my life. To my spiritual father, Dr. James Maloney, his wife, Joy, and their son, Andrew, who brought me into their family, loved me as a son, and showed me what is possible in the Kingdom of God, and to imitate Christ. To my friend and counselor, Bill Ollendike, who demonstrated God's heart to me and my wife. To my friend, Brian Fraley, who sharpens me like iron, and whose friendship I could not be without: we have faced many battles together and have always had each other's backs. To the giants of the faith who have inspired and encouraged me: Bill Johnson, Dr. Randy Clark, Chris Gore, Paul Martini, Michael Dalton, and Richie Seltzer. Thank you all so much for endorsing this book; I am grateful to know you.

CONTENTS

	Foreword *by Dr. James Maloney*	1
INTRODUCTION	The Importance of Healing	5
CHAPTER 1	The Girl Who Grew	11
CHAPTER 2	Gloriously Ruined	17
CHAPTER 3	Take It Fast!	21
CHAPTER 4	Past Tense	27
CHAPTER 5	Jesus the Breaker	31
CHAPTER 6	The Revelation of Faith	35
CHAPTER 7	Moments of Boom!	41
CHAPTER 8	The Conviction of Faith	47
CHAPTER 9	Historical Significance	53
CHAPTER 10	Take It by Force	59
CHAPTER 11	This Time It's Personal!	65
CHAPTER 12	We're Dead	69
CHAPTER 13	Cultivating Sensitivity	75
CHAPTER 14	It's Relational	81
CHAPTER 15	How Faith Operates	87
CHAPTER 16	Stepping into Faith	93
CHAPTER 17	Seizing the Moment	97
CHAPTER 18	I Also Imitate Christ	103
CHAPTER 19	A Constant Shift	109

CHAPTER 20 Moved with Compassion 115
CHAPTER 21 Tossing Out Junk and Expressing Love. . . . 121
CHAPTER 22 The Way Jesus Did It 127
CHAPTER 23 Now It's Our Turn 133
CHAPTER 24 Brazil 139
CHAPTER 25 Branham's Pulls 143
CHAPTER 26 The Man with No Tongue 147
CHAPTER 27 Don't Live a Two-Thirds Life 153
CHAPTER 28 Two-Thirds Is Antichrist 159
CHAPTER 29 The Exposure of the Spirit 165
CHAPTER 30 Facing Rejection. 171
CHAPTER 31 Strengthen the Inner Man 175

FOREWORD

I believe that in the next ten to fifteen years, should the Lord tarry, we will see remarkable expressions of God's supernatural power, through His people, in geographical locations all over the earth. While I am not an ultra-dominionist in my philosophy and theology, I am convinced that as deep darkness covers the face of the earth (and indeed, it is and will continue to do so), the Lord will arise over us, His children, and His glory will be seen upon us in marvelous ways (see Isa. 60:2).

Specifically, one of these expressions I am firmly persuaded the Lord has spoken of will be the hallmark of the forthcoming Dove Company, which I've talked and written so much about. This Company, a segment of the Lord's Army, is being prepared even now to move in a powerful blending of the prophetic seer and healing anointings. Our ministry, Dove on the Rise International, is one (of many) of these voices of healing that the Lord is using as forerunners of this great move that is fast approaching.

As a board member and executive associate evangelist of Dove on the Rise International, Dr. John Proodian is one of these voices. His book, *Accelerated Healing*, is speaking directly to this exciting increase in miraculous healing that we believe is swiftly coming to the forefront of the Body of Christ. (Not that it hasn't been prevalent in times past; I just perceive we're approaching a special dispensation of that gracing on a larger scale as we approach these "end times," whatever that happens to mean.)

It has been my honor and privilege to see John explode into his own expression of God's healing ministry in the several years we've traveled together. I'm so excited to see this passion reproduced within the next generation, which, in turn, is now being reproduced within the next generation (these so-called Millennials who will be the main force in this Dove Company in the next decade or so). What has taken me forty years to develop (not that I have attained—I've still much to learn!) John has seen accelerated and "downloaded" in his own expression in the last seven or eight years, and I think what he is reproducing in others will be even more greatly accelerated. It's the "snowball rolling down the mountain" effect. What my generation developed over a lifetime of ministry will take a decade in the next, and in the next one beyond that, just a few years. Our ceiling of expression becomes their floorboard—and that's the whole point! I can't wait to see it!

It's humbling to have a role to play in this generational expansion; and while I'm happy to call myself a "father" now—such as I am—in this forerunning group, I'm actually more excited to see what happens in the "sons and daughters." I get a real kick out of it!

Books like *Accelerated Healing* are important because they provide a link between generations—mine to John's, and John's to the Millennials'. It's a progression, see. Through his honest and unassuming testimony, John starts off with how things should not be done in the name of healing ministry; but he quickly progresses into the good news of how things should be done to see this manifestation of God's healing grace take root in church culture at large. There are several simple, yet important, key truths that you can adapt in your own walk and ministry expression. Yes, even the so-called "laypeople" have a ministry expression. If you're born again, God has something for you to do; and only you can do it, because you're the only "you" on the planet!

Here's what I love about this book:

1. It's chock full of testimony—from John and his wife directly, and others who've been touched by his ministry—people saying, "Hey, this worked for me. It can work for you too."
2. It's not difficult to understand. The prophetic healing expression is supposed to be easy enough for anyone to grasp, not just a few "special" scholarly people—you don't have to speak ancient Greek and Hebrew to "get it." John writes conversationally, and I love that!
3. It presents timely, scriptural truths you can implement in your day-to-day life to see an acceleration of the healing anointing wedded to a prophetic unction so that you can touch the people around you, wherever you are.

What's not to love here? You've done well, picking up this book, and I encourage you to take the time to read it through more than once—let it settle in your spirit and cultivate a passion—like John's, like mine—to see the Lord accelerate healing in your life and the lives of those He puts you into contact with. Seize the day!

—Dr. James Maloney

President, Dove on the Rise International

Author, *The Dancing Hand of God, The Panoramic Seer, Overwhelmed by the Spirit*, and more

INTRODUCTION

THE IMPORTANCE OF HEALING

We have a tendency in the Charismatic circles to overlook the absolutely life-changing principle of receiving a healing from God. It's not that we're unappreciative or unthankful, but I often think we don't fully understand the ramifications of how a healing—no matter how small—forever alters the life of the person who received that healing. We may see someone's big toe get healed, and we say, "Praise God! Isn't He good? That was neat."

However, the person whose toe was healed has now had an encounter—a brush with almighty God who has touched them in a supernatural and personal way. It goes far beyond just the toe being healed, as "neat" as that is. That person and those standing around have just encountered a signpost in their lives that says, "I, the Lord your God, am here, and I care about your physical well-being—even your toe!"

We need to have a greater revelation of just how awesome it is when the Lord touches a person physically—our lives should never be the same! Our lives need to be completely different from that moment forward after the personal demonstration of God's goodness.

All miracles should be life-changing, whether it be a shoulder restored to proper function or a lame person rising up and walking—it is the same God performing a miracle that, in the natural, could never occur. *Every* healing should be celebrated, no matter how "small" we think it is. The bottom line is, we should thank God that *any* of us are healed, because no healing is small. It is all a manifestation of God's power over His creation, and that deserves our thanksgiving!

When my wife's knee was healed, we decided to be those kinds of Christians who rejoice and give thanks in everything!

As God's sons and daughters, we should all desire the same thing—to see people saved, healed, and delivered. That really should be the primary focus in all our lives—releasing the Kingdom inside us so that people can enter into that Kingdom, touch that Kingdom for themselves, and be transformed.

Healing is my passion. I absolutely *love* seeing the Lord break into someone's life and restructure something in their body that was wrong. However, as I often say, up until an encounter when my wife's knee was healed, there had been about a thirty-year period during which I considered myself "God's least anointed" person.

After my dad died, I ended up being part of a healing team and thinking, "Please don't get in *my* prayer line!" Not out of fear, because I desperately wanted to see the people healed, but I knew they wouldn't get healed coming to me. How is *that* for super faith?

I'd pray for people; they'd die. It was so painful to pray for the sick and not see anything happen. Such a sad thing. I knew that it was *me*, that the problem was me, but I didn't know how to fix *me*.

I hear of people who have healing ministries talk about how, before they received a fuller revelation of God's healing grace, they prayed for people without seeing many results. Some have said it took them ten years, some maybe only six months. I often think facetiously, "Lightweights." It was almost three decades of frustration before I was finally able to "get" the concept, at least in some way, of how the Lord operates in healing—and His passionate desire to see people healed *quickly*.

It was my fault, of course, not God's—His timeframe would've been significantly hastened, as this book will try to show. But praise God I'm wasting no more time in presenting the truth to people that He does indeed heal, and He desires to do it *now*. Not some far-distant time in the future. The Lord, in His infinite love and grace, showed me just how insistent and uncompromising He is concerning healing His children speedily.

But before that powerful revelation came, I watched as my dad developed cancer and slowly withered away. He moved from a cane to a walker to a wheelchair; then he was bedbound, where he slipped into a coma, then died. It was about the worst death I could've imagined—someone I loved so much, seeing him suffer. It was such a painful period of my life, and I think a part of me died when he did—a part that *needed* to die, the part that said, "I can do nothing to fix this." I was obviously living in deception, confusion, and blindness, but it's hard to *see* the goodness of God in those kinds of situations, and it created a wounding that needed to be healed.

It was through God's grace that He brought spiritual giants into my life who *knew* about how healing was supposed to work—my spiritual father James Maloney, Randy Clark, Bill Johnson, and many others. People who also had experienced failure in praying for the sick and had "dug it out"—the truth that God was healing people today. They were used by the Lord to resurrect that part of me that died into a newness of life, a passion, and a purpose to set my forehead as a flint and say, "I *can* be used by God to see people healed." They instilled within me a glimmer of hope right at a time I was considering turning away from it. Not turning away from God, you understand, but the truth that He had a covenantal, burning desire to heal people in this day and age. The power that my soul (mind, will, and emotions) had over me was broken; I became renewed in my thinking, and I was able finally to allow my spirit to rise up and reach out to *the* Spirit to see His power manifested for healing.

The moment when my wife Janet's knee was touched, that was the signpost that forever altered the course of our lives. I remember so distinctly the very first time I got a word of knowledge for someone and they were healed. Think about what that was like. Thirty years of fruitless frustration all washed away in a moment. All the emotional pain draining out of me as physical pain drained out that person's body—we were both touched at that precise moment. I thought to myself, *Finally! God, healing is here!* The ecstasy of seeing God just be who He is, to see His goodness manifested—I was gloriously ruined!

I have learned that "dealing with disappointment" (whatever that entails) does *not* get rid of disappointment. No matter how hard we try to "get over it," it doesn't work. We were not created to deal with disappointment; we were created for victory! I had tried for years to make healing "work," thinking, *This time will be different.* But it never was.

Now I am firmly persuaded that the only way to deal with disappointment is to get victory in the area you need. To overcome the disappointment of not receiving healing, one must receive that healing—it proves the authority of Jesus and heals the hurts of previous letdowns. We cannot talk away the problem; the problem must be solved.

Now, because the "testimony of Jesus is the spirit of prophecy" (Rev. 19:10), I want this book to be just that—a testimony of healing, mixed with some of the revelation God has been gracious enough to give to me since that life-altering encounter. I pray that you will be able to adapt it into your life in order to receive the same "newness of life" that I did. To come to a greater understanding that Jesus heals *now*—His yesterday (the work of the cross) is to be brought into our today at this *kairos* moment. It's exciting! It is the Kingdom of God in expression.

In an effort to help facilitate that Kingdom expression in your life—at least in some small way—this book is a teaching on creative miracles, the gift of faith, and the "Third Pull of the Spirit," as some theologians have termed the coming move of God. I will only teach what I have learned and experienced personally regarding the gift of faith—nothing speculative or in theory, only things I have seen practiced in my own life.

We all love creative miracles, don't we? I am convinced that God loves working miraculously even more than we enjoy receiving His miracles. I believe that is true, so if you need to receive healing in your body, permit the material here to encourage your faith to receive that healing as you read this book. I expect God will heal you as you read some of the testimonies in this book—I have seen Him work this way many times, which is why I have included these testimonies here. Not to boast in myself, but to encourage *your* faith to receive a similar touch from the Lord yourself.

CHAPTER 1

THE GIRL WHO GREW

The first time I saw Dr. James Maloney was in Pennsylvania in 2010, and he was talking about all the miracles he'd seen—crazy stuff like pacemakers dissolving and disappearing and hearts getting healed, incredible stuff like metal dissolving out of people's bodies—and my wife and I were sitting near the back, almost salivating. I remember thinking, *This is everything I've dreamed about!*

He started explaining this "panoramic operation" that he operates in, where he'll call someone up, hold them by the right hand with his right hand, and proceed to describe an open, what he calls "panoramic," vision. Very clearly, specific details of this person's life will appear, similar to a movie. I've witnessed this operation many times, and the level of detail is mind blowing. Things like, "I see you—you're about eleven years old, and you're in the bathroom. I see you slipped on a rug that had water underneath it, and you hit your head, right here, on the back of the tub. It was a blue rug."

That kind of very specific operation raises the level of faith in the room so that multiple miracles will take place. Not only does the person he's ministering to get healed, but the level of corporate faith hits the roof. I believe we are entering deeper into a season with these kinds of operations. There is such a resting of His glory that miracles become extremely easy to receive. That's the way I like it. I like it easy, not hard; don't you?

James called a school-aged girl to come forward in front of the congregation. She was probably somewhere between ten and twelve years of age, but she was the size of a five- or six-year-old. I don't remember the specific medical condition she had, some kind of chromosomal defect perhaps, but it caused her growth to be severely stunted. I'd estimate she was about half the size she should've been.

James went into the panoramic operation and named this girl's exact condition. He then said, "And God has healed you of this condition." I remember thinking, *Praise God, that's awesome!*

He went on to say to this little girl, "God has just told me He's going to restore your stature as well." Upon hearing this, I thought, *How cool! Well, praise God!* believing that, who knows, over the years, someday, she's going to be a normal height.

But then James said, "Oh, God told me He's gonna restore your stature right now!"

Now, how many know it's game on when someone makes a statement like that? To let those kinds of words come out of your mouth publicly takes a significant level of faith.

My wife and I said to each other, "I gotta see this!" so we ran down to the front. It had already gotten crowded down there by this time. James put his hand on the little girl's head; she was about at the height of his belt buckle. He told everyone just to worship the Lord—everyone focus on God, not on this.

(I've been trying to learn this from him, and now I'm trying to pass it on to others—keep the focus on Him, not on the problem. When we focus on the problem, we've got "the problem." When we focus on the solution, we've got "the Solution." Just worship the Lord—let it be about Him, not what needs to be fixed.)

Behold, this little girl started stretching right in front of our eyes! It was one of the craziest moments that changed my life completely. She just started stretching up to James' shirt button; then she grew up to the next button, and so on. Of course, everyone was freaking out! At the end, her pant legs were several inches shorter. Later, we heard she'd grown five inches within minutes.

Those are the kinds of miracles that you dream about! That's just like *living* the Gospels to me—Book of Acts kinds of things. My wife and I had been wanting to see miracles like that our whole lives. And you know, when you see something like that, your life is never the same. How do you respond to something like that? How can you go on with "life as normal" after you've seen someone get touched in that kind of a profound way? Talk about a paradigm shift!

You can never stay at the same level of faith when you've experienced something like that. Right there, I told the Lord, *I will give my life for this. This is what I want my life to be about, God. I want to see the manifestation of Your goodness in this way consistently!*

Just witnessing those miracles broke a stronghold of unbelief for healing. It started changing me into a different person spiritually. My prayers changed, shifting into prayers of faith.

After that miracle, when we returned to the hotel that night, I remember praying for a man who had had no feeling in his arm, down to his hand, for twenty-six years. When I prayed for him, God totally healed his arm, and the man gave his life to the Lord! Something had changed!

So often, the Israelites lived in fear—fear of enemies, fear of failure, fear of famine, whatever. In the end, that was all unbelief. But when David stood up and slew Goliath, something broke in the nation; they were empowered. They started slaying their own giants as well! But it wouldn't have happened if they hadn't witnessed one man stepping out in faith!

It's hard to travel, to be away from my wife and children. But it is worth it to see the look on people's faces when they have an encounter with the Lord. They're healed and set free.

It starts with a stirring in your heart, beyond just a spiritual hunger—you see people getting healed, you see the impact it has on their lives, you see people having encounters with God, and you long for it yourself. "I want what these people have! Lord, pour me out like You pour out these ministers." I remember Randy Clark once saying, "Like a coin in Your pocket, Lord, spend me!"

Honestly, after seeing these kinds of manifestations, nothing else is worth living for. Only having these kinds of encounters with the Lord, having such a relationship with Him that He pours Himself out through you so that others can encounter Him as well—that's what it's all about.

I had the privilege of traveling with Dr. Maloney on nearly every trip about a year after seeing the girl grow, and I've never once looked back. My life has been too drastically changed to ever go back. I've seen the most amazing miracles, too many to even categorize. Metal dissolving, whole body parts growing back—*those* kinds of creative miracles. And I know it's only going to escalate—His presence, His peace, and His glory coming upon us in ever increasing waves. Even after all I've seen, I believe we're just getting warmed up. The best is still yet to come—praise the Lord!

CHAPTER 2

GLORIOUSLY RUINED

I enjoy sharing testimonies of healing that demonstrate God's supreme goodness and how His Holy Spirit moves in our lives. I believe it is through this sharing that the Holy Spirit is given rein to show His glory in greater and greater measure as we honor how He moves in each one of us. It encourages our faith to hear of God moving in His children's lives.

Every healing is an amazing demonstration of God's goodness and love manifested toward us. The reason we are able to expect to see a healing accelerated in our lives is based upon the foundation of God's love toward humanity. It is from the bedrock of love that Jesus proceeded to ratify a new Covenant in His own blood, which includes the gift of bodily healing.

Every healing is special to me because so few people got healed when I prayed for them before. Thirty years I lived like that! My father passed away while I was struggling to stand in faith for his healing—it was devastating at the time. In truth, it was a real low kind of faith based only on sincere desire, which is not the biblical kind of faith. His passing was such a blow that whatever kind of "faith" I had simply evaporated in the disappointment and grief.

But over a decade ago, my wife, Janet, was in an accident, and her knee was damaged as a result. A few years later, while attending a conference where Bill Johnson was speaking, a word of knowledge went forth about her situation. At that time, her knee was radically touched, and that singular occurrence is what started us both down the path of pursuing the knowledge and manifestation of the truth—that God heals today, wants to heal people today, and is asking us to press in with all haste into receiving that healing.

My wife and I for a long time hadn't walked in these kinds of miraculous displays of God's power. We started hearing about ministers like Bill Johnson and Randy Clark, and I ordered a bunch of their books. Janet and I devoured each one, and it became clear to us that we *had* to go see ministers like this in operation.

Our first meeting, we drove several hours to attend a Bill Johnson conference. I remember what he was talking about the first time I heard him speak; I was thinking, *This is it! This is what I've been waiting for my whole life! This is the way it's supposed to be.* You know, your heart gets stirred at these kinds of events. You have a distinct revelation where you realize your life is never going to be the same, but at the same time you realize you've been a bit of a "Christian idiot" for a number of years as well. That part was hard for me to deal with, like, *What have I been doing before this point? What a waste!*

Bill gave a word of knowledge—somebody in this room was in an accident more than ten years ago and is still suffering the effects of that.

My wife leaped up like a spring, not one bit of hesitation, and this is one of the keys to accelerating healing—don't hesitate, go for it! Don't question it at all.

Janet's knee had been crushed between two cars, years before. There had been severe swelling, and then it was getting better for a while, but then it just got worse to the point that it was chronic. She couldn't walk for very long without the knee getting all puffy, and she would likely need knee replacement surgery. The procedure was going to be costly, and we were going to have to sell our house and purchase a one-story home because of the difficulty she had going up and down stairs.

But here at this conference, when Bill gave the word of knowledge, she leaped up and exclaimed, "That's for me!"

Bill said, "Somebody put a hand on that lady," and she felt the power of God hit her, and the rest of that night she felt a tingling all the way down her calf. God completely reconstructed her knee. She had chronic pain every day up to that point. From that day on, she has had no pain at all in that knee. Praise God!

That moment of her encounter was wonderful, and she and I will never forget it the rest of our lives. But it's the "after story" that really shows the changes in our lives. What comes after an encounter like that? How do you respond to such a miracle? Well, for ourselves, I can honestly say it completely transformed our lives.

Ever since I've known my wife she's been a devout woman, but her relationship with God just went to another level after that—seeking Him, sharing about Him with other people. A stranger can't talk to my wife for more than a couple minutes without hearing about her knee getting healed. She just tells everybody about it. Some people think she's crazy, like, "Who is this weird lady?" But some people are completely fascinated, and she's gotten to pray for many of them and seen many, many people healed.

It's lead her into ministering in the prophetic and training and activating others to hear God and be led by the Spirit—open doors here in the States and overseas that we never dreamed would be available to us. God's pouring himself out through Janet out all over the place, all stemming from this miracle!

Praise the Lord! She and I were gloriously ruined by that one encounter. I believe a similar "ruining" will happen to you as well if the Lord has not already done so. That's why I'm sharing these testimonies—not to boast as someone "special" but to show I believe these kinds of miraculous quickenings of the Lord are equally available to all His saints.

CHAPTER 3

TAKE IT FAST!

I had a significant dream wherein God showed me ministering in front of a group of people in a word of knowledge operation. After letting that flow forth, the Spirit started "highlighting" people in the audience, lighting them up one after the other. So I began to acknowledge these people: "You are being 'highlighted' by God."

As soon as I said that, it was like the people were in water. Not falling into water, but it was like they were surrounded by water—kind of difficult to describe. But I said to them, "Test it out," and as they began to stretch forth their limbs in faith—or whatever area they needed healing in—they would be spontaneously healed. It was happening all over the auditorium—such a powerful manifestation!

But then I looked down at myself and saw that one of my legs was horribly mangled and twisted, and I exclaimed in shock, "Oh, God, I need healing too!" I felt the tangible presence of the healing anointing strike my leg, and I heard these words from the Lord: *"Take it fast!"*

So I immediately stretched out my leg, and it was made whole. I started rejoicing before the Lord, and then I came out of the dream. I asked the Lord, "What did that mean?" (Seems like a relevant question, right?)

He said, "I want you train My people to take it fast." In the context of receiving healing from Him, He was saying, "Take it fast! My people are receiving healing too slowly. I want you to teach them to receive from Me *now*." We need to take it quickly, move forward speedily, press into *now*. It is the violent who take it by force! (See Matthew 11:12.)

When we "take it fast," all we are doing is receiving healing from the Healer, moving to Him as quickly as we can with an expectation that our Father *wants* to heal us. It really means "take *Him* fast." It is God's very nature to be the Healer, so we are simply taking more of Him.

The Lord was showing me that *hesitation is one of the opposites of faith*. We need to be taught not to hesitate in any situation, specifically healing. Proverbs 28:1 tells us that the godly are as "bold as a lion." Hebrews 4:16 admonishes us to "come boldly to the throne of grace."

A lot of times, well-meaning Christians hesitate when they want to receive from God—either out of a misconception that they're being humble and contrite or out of a lack of understanding that God is equally available to *all* His children. He accepts each one of us *now* just as openly as He accepts Jesus. The only reason you weren't saved a year earlier is because *you* kept God waiting. It's a similar notion to healing. It is there *now* and always has been in your lifetime. God isn't waiting to heal you—you're waiting to receive it. So why not take it fast?

I hear many excuses. For example, we'll have a word of knowledge, say, about an injured thumb—down by the knuckle, perhaps—and the person out there with the hurt thumb *hesitates*. "Well, it's not *that* area of my thumb that hurts—it's up by the fingernail! That word must not be for me." They debate with themselves. "That sounds like my condition, except it's not *exactly* my condition, so I am not sure that word is for me." That's hesitation. It is *not* taking it fast! Make sure you don't talk yourself out of a miracle!

If a word of knowledge goes forth for a specific purpose, that obviously means the presence of God is there for healing, so we should be clamoring to receive it—*fast!* It's like we want to be 100 percent sure that God is saying, "Here is healing!" before we act on it. The truth is, it's already 100 percent sure and was 100 percent sure before you were even born. You *were* healed by the atonement of the cross some 2,000 years ago (see 1 Pet. 2:24). We shouldn't need to be convinced God wants us healed. We should be taking our healing by force—*now!*

The earthly ministry of the Lord confirms this—He healed anyone and everyone who came to Him in some level of faith. Healing was never withheld. Now, this doesn't negate the necessity of getting confirmation from the written Word concerning, say, a dream or a vision—something subjective that's not expressly detailed in the Bible. Of course we need discernment. But when it comes to our covenant rights (and healing is in the New Covenant!), we don't need to debate with ourselves if God wants to heal us.

Any word from the Lord can be applied to us. If God says one person is being healed, all of us can be healed. If the minister says,

"There is a person here with a tumor in their stomach," He wants to heal you of your heart disease too! He is no respecter of persons (see Acts 10:34; Rom. 2:11 KJV).

When the presence of the Lord is there to heal, of necessity that means He wants *every single person* in that place healed. But see, we often hesitate. "Is that for me too? He said stomach tumors. Is God healing heart disease?" The answer is yes—don't wait another second to take your healing!

A single word of knowledge for an individual person can lead to a corporate breakthrough, raising the level of faith for the entire congregation to receive from the Lord. Even out there in the marketplace, when others witness a timely word of knowledge for one person that brings healing, it can lead to a breakthrough in the public setting. It's not just for within the four walls of the church!

When my wife's knee got healed, she took it fast! She leaped up and grabbed it by faith, reached for it with both hands as quickly as she could! She didn't hesitate one moment!

Keep in mind, that's not to say there is no progression in healing. There is a process of recovery—not every healing is the workings of miracles. In the Greek, there are three words used for healing—*sozo* (Strong's G4982), *therapeuo* (Strong's G2323), and *iaomai* (Strong's G2390).

Sozo implies salvation, rescuing, restoration for all three components of a human being—spirit, soul, and body. Most of the time this is translated as "save," but a few times it is translated as "heal."

Therapeuo is used to mean "cure." This is where we get our word *therapy*. It speaks of gifts of healings (notice they are plural; there are many ways the Lord heals, and these are almost always a process). The vast majority of times this word is used in the New Testament, it is translated "heal."

Iaomai is an instant miracle of healing. It means to heal by one way and one way only—miraculous power. When this word is used, it's almost exclusively translated "heal" and encompasses a release of God's anointing and authority (especially over the demonic) to perform a miracle of healing. This is primarily how Jesus operated in His earthly ministry.

It would be wonderful if all healing was *iaomai*, but we cannot neglect the other forms of healing. However, even if we are dealing with a *therapeuo* healing, we need to receive it instantly, just like *iaomai*. It is our attitude toward healing that must be refashioned. We're not working to get God to heal us; we're learning to receive it *quickly*. Even if the full manifestation is a process, we receive every healing immediately—we need to take it fast!

This was the case with the woman with the issue of blood (see Matt. 9; Mark 5; Luke 8) and also with blind Bartimaeus (see Mark 10). They didn't hesitate. These are examples of people who *jumped* at the opportunity to receive from God. The Bible is full of stories of people laying hold of the Kingdom without hesitating.

I don't see any waiting around for healing in the ministry of Jesus in the Gospels. It was 100 percent, all the time, for every person who came to Him in some level of faith—even imperfect faith. He wanted them healed, and He wanted them healed *now*, not later.

It is *forceful* men and women who lay hold of the Kingdom. It's a scriptural principle: "And from the days of John the Baptist until now the kingdom of heaven suffers violence, and the violent take it by force" (Matt. 11:12).

Don't misunderstand—it's not being forceful with *God*. He is not moved by a sense of aggression from us toward Him. When I mention that the woman with the issue of blood was forceful or

Blind Bartimaeus was forceful, I mean it is about being forceful against the things that *keep* you from God and from having an encounter with Him.

The woman forced her way through the culture of her world in order to get to Jesus. She was unclean and should not have been touching anyone; she had many things against her, and many things in her current world system that told her not to do what she did. But she did it anyway and forced her way through all the rules of her time in order to get to Jesus and be made whole. Nothing would stop her!

This is the attitude of resolve we are talking about, and this is having faith so strong you force your way through any hindrances that would keep you from taking what Jesus is offering *now*.

CHAPTER 4

PAST TENSE

Most of us know the truth that Jesus *already* provided (past tense) our healing over 2,000 years ago on the cross (see Isa. 53:5; 1 Pet. 2:24). It is a done deal. However, many of us struggle with procuring what happened in the past for our present situations. It doesn't change the fact that God's time to heal was *before*, and we need to step into it *now*.

The concept of *acceleration* is the act on our part of bringing God's yesterday into our today. He wanted us healed a long time ago. Israel, when they entered the Promised Land to possess it, was forty years off from God's original timing. We need to "catch up" to what God has already done!

Once you feel God, or if you even *think* God is doing something, take it fast and be healed, *right now*, even as you're reading *in this moment*. Once the healing has manifested, acknowledge what God is doing in your life by praising and thanking Him.

We need to be taught that the split second we feel *any* connection with the Lord, any download of faith, any amount of anointing, any amount of His presence, corporately or personally—*boom!*—snatch it fast, grab hold of it quickly, and don't let it go for anything in the world. *Take Him fast!* We need to be like striking lightning when it comes to taking healing from the Lord. Pounce on it like a tiger and shake it with our teeth! Scarf it down like a hungry kid on a cheeseburger. (Did that give a good word picture in your mind?)

We don't need to wait for some time that God wants to heal us. His yesterday needs to be brought into our today. "Now is the day of salvation" (2 Cor. 6:2). *Now* now—right now, not later. Salvation, as I'm sure you're aware, is an all-inclusive word that means whole salvation, spirit, soul, and body. Do a word study on *sozo* if you don't believe me. We can just as properly substitute the word *healing* in every case of *salvation* or put in *healed* for *saved*. They are identical renderings because the Greek word means total salvation for every facet of our existence.

The purpose of this material is not to convince a disbeliever that Jesus heals today, but as an aside I'd like to point out that "healing" is just as much for the body and the mind as for the spirit (the born-again experience). Technically, our spirit isn't "healed," per se, when we are born again—it is recreated, made alive toward God once again. But when Isaiah 53:4-5 talks about griefs and sorrows (literally "sicknesses" and "pains" in the Hebrew; look them up in a concordance)—the "by His stripes we are healed" *is* talking about your earthly body and soul (again—the mind, will, and emotions.)

So because this passage of Scripture is speaking of the crucifixion of Christ, this is all a past-tense situation, a done deal. God's time to heal you was *yesterday*. You need to bring that revelation into your *today*. Accelerate the speed at which you are receiving from the Lord. That's the thrust of this book—to show you that the healing you need is yours for the taking *already*.

There's a biblical principle to this concept that God has *already* accomplished something we need to enter into *now*. For example, the Israelites didn't enter into the Promised Land until forty years *later* than God intended. Their inheritance was supposed to be received *at that time*, but hesitation and unbelief hindered God's *now* plan for four decades. They wandered around in the wilderness when God had planned for them to take possession of the land at that moment.

Your provision of healing isn't something that is coming to you in the future. It was there before you were. What we need to do is take yesterday's truth and make it today's reality. I have been guilty of praying too many wimpy prayers over the years that were rooted in a hesitant attitude. I am sure I cannot be the only one who's done this—otherwise, everyone would already be healed, and we wouldn't need books like this.

We need to know healing is here, now; it's already done. This is an absolute truth, not open for discussion. According to 1 Peter 2:24, you were already healed when Jesus received the stripes upon His back. I think many charismatic Christians believe this on some level, but clearly it is not quite the reality in their daily lives for those who "struggle" to receive a healing.

Like when you ask your boss, "When do you want this?" and he or she says, "Yesterday." Right? God is like that. When does He want you to receive your healing? Yesterday. It was already done. He is already so far ahead of you that your healing was procured before the foundation of the world (see Rev. 13:8).

One of the problems that can arise from trying to put healing as a present-tense thing ("We are trying to get this person healed") is that we can actually pray *past* the point of healing. When I feel healing virtue go out, I stop praying for the healing to manifest and simply acknowledge that virtue has gone forth. I don't want to keep praying for that same thing. Otherwise what I'm really saying is, "Maybe it hasn't really happened," if I keep praying for healing beyond when it has already occurred. That takes the emphasis off the healing *already* happening more than 2,000 years ago.

Jesus' healing anointing is just as strong and valid and operative today as it was when He walked this earth. However, it is our response to that anointing, or rather our lack of dwelling in His glory, that can be a hindrance to taking Him fast. Let's discuss Jesus's breaker anointing for a bit.

CHAPTER 5

JESUS THE BREAKER

We all need to pursue an ever-deepening resting of God's glory on our lives and ministries. Certainly none of us has arrived, and there are more levels to God's glory than we could even fathom, but the pursuit is still there—that driving force to see God move more and more powerfully.

I remember a meeting in Australia where James Maloney had to shut down the healing portion of the meeting. I believe a man had come up with a missing leg. And James was honest. He said, "You know, we need more glory for these kinds of miracles you're asking for." There is a principle in that—none of us has gotten to that point, and to a certain extent I'm not sure it's even possible without the Lord's sovereign choice of bestowing grace upon us, where we see *everything* we want to see. But that doesn't stop us pressing in for more.

We know with Jesus it's all the same—it's not any harder for Him to grow back a limb than to heal a head cold. Makes no difference to Him—He's the Healer, and any kind of miraculous expression is easy for Him. It's all the same.

But Jesus, in His infinite wisdom, has chosen to work alongside people like you and me who have not reached the level of perspective that our Lord has. Our human natures—which we are all somewhere in the process of changing to become more and more like Christ's nature—make a bigger deal out of some of these things than He would as the Healer. The key is to keep pursuing that level of Christ's perspective concerning healing.

I remember the next night in Australia, we started seeing more glory as we pressed into worshiping and focusing on Jesus, and then we started seeing great breakthroughs in healing and miracles, signs, and wonders.

There is a principle here for our lives as well. We need to press into a "resting" of Jesus' glory—a thickening, so to speak, of His powerful worth in every aspect of our lives. As that anointing is cultivated and deepened, accelerated healing cannot help but be a byproduct of that time invested waiting upon the Lord in high praise and worship.

What we're talking about here, this resting glory, is actually a thickening, for lack of a better word, of the anointing that God has placed in each born-again spirit.

Isaiah 10:27 says, "It shall come to pass in that day that his burden will be taken away from your shoulder, and his yoke from your neck, and the yoke will be destroyed because of the anointing oil."

I've experienced this anointing a great deal working and serving alongside Dr. Maloney and others. They each carry a mantle of anointing that has been "thickened" over the course of their lives as they've dedicated their entire existence to seeing that anointing break the yokes of bondage that weigh down so many people.

Maybe there's someone who's been prayed for many times but so far hasn't experienced that yoke being broken. Then one day, in a meeting sitting under an anointed minister of God, they suddenly receive the manifestation they were seeking. Why? What changed? There is a breaker anointing on certain people who have walked in this "accelerated healing" for a while. But it's available to all of us, you know? The Bible says these signs shall follow all who believe (see Mark 16:17). Jesus said we shall lay hands on the sick, and they shall recover. That's for everybody; can we agree on that? Amen?

We cannot misinterpret the epistles in a way that contradicts the Gospels. Here's an example of what that would be. We interpret Paul's writings about "gifts of healing" and say, "I don't have gifts of healing; therefore, I cannot see people get healed." We've just contradicted the words of Jesus by interpreting the epistles that way.

Our interpretation of the epistles cannot contradict the reality of Jesus, the ministry of Jesus. It has to be about Jesus, Jesus, Jesus, Jesus. We have to read the letters to the churches in the context of the life and ministry of Jesus. Otherwise we're probably going to misinterpret what Paul or Peter is saying.

It is very important to interpret everything we read in the Bible through the life and ministry of Jesus Christ—He *is* the Word, the sum total of everything God has ever thought about humanity. It all rests in His Son. If we do not interpret the written Word through *the* Word (Jesus, the *Logos* of God), we can very easily explain away all that happened in the Gospels. I'm convinced this is how people become cessationists (and similar theological ideologies)—through a misinterpretation of the epistles. Cessationism isn't based upon the scriptures in the Gospels—they believe Jesus did all that stuff the Gospels say, only He doesn't do it now. Except the Bible says Jesus Christ is the same yesterday, today, and forever (see Heb. 13:8). So when they read the epistles, they come to the misinformed conclusion that sometime after Peter and Paul and the others, Jesus stopped operating like He did in the Gospels.

But I'm not here to argue against cessationism. I want to talk about Jesus, the Originator of this "breaker anointing."

Accelerated healing must be about Jesus. It always has to be about the Lord and giving Him the glory. My perspective on healing and the gifts in operation today is pretty simple—I know that it's Him; it's just Him, and we as ministers are simply conduits to help connect others to Him.

Really, all miraculous power is just a celebration of Jesus, and that anointing manifests in people's lives as we celebrate an unchanging, all-powerful Christ and Lord. Healing is supposed to be fun, not drudgery. I think that's one of the prime components to deepening, or thickening, this breaker anointing in our lives—to simply enjoy and celebrate the power of Jesus. If we really believed His power was in our spirits, we couldn't help but celebrate, and it would make "trying to get healed" a lot easier. One of the hindrances to this is a lack of revelation of faith.

CHAPTER 6

THE REVELATION OF FAITH

There are three phases, or levels, of faith—we'll discuss them throughout this book, but for now, the first phase is *revelation*. Accelerated healing is quickened when you and I get a revelation of God, of who He is, and of His goodness. I love the story in Acts 14.

We see Paul here preaching, and there is a certain man from Lystra; we don't know the man's name, but he's listening to Paul speaking "Kingdom words." The apostle is operating in the power of the Spirit at this moment, and the man is receiving revelation. Something amazing happens.

> *And in Lystra a certain man without strength in his feet was sitting, a cripple from his mother's womb, who had never walked. This man heard Paul speaking. Paul, observing him intently and seeing that he had faith to be healed, said with a loud voice, "Stand up straight on your feet!" And he leaped and walked* (Acts 14:8-10).

So here is this man, crippled from birth, hearing Paul speak. Let's picture this scene. What's happening here? Paul is speaking words of Kingdom life about the Kingdom of Jesus and about the way this Kingdom functions. Romans 10:17 states that "faith comes by hearing, and hearing by the word of God." The man begins to connect to Jesus the Healer through the words that Paul is speaking, and the apostle is able to see that this guy is engaging; he sees an element of faith, right?

Who says faith can't be seen? We always hear it stated that faith can't be seen, but this passage says Paul saw that the man had faith.

So faith *can* be seen in some instances, and this is one of them. I've seen faith on people, and Jesus said to some people, "Your faith has made you well." We know He didn't say that to everybody; there must have been something the Lord was able to perceive.

Obviously people came to the Lord with varying levels of faith. The leper in Mark 1 said, "If You are willing..." whereas the woman with the issue of blood came with a *lot* of faith, as did the centurion whose servant was dying. There are different levels of faith, but it's important to point out they all got healed anyway—even Lazarus who, being *dead*, probably didn't have a lot of faith.

In the passage of Acts 14, Paul sees faith rising in that moment, and when he sees that he's able to make that bold declaration: "Stand up! Get on your feet!" And the man is made whole. See how it's all about initiating an encounter? The Kingdom words that Paul was speaking enabled that crippled man to have an encounter with God. We too are to be conduits for connection.

Let's say, for example, I get a word of knowledge for something, and I say, "God wants to heal someone's right shoulder today. I think someone hurt it in an accident three years ago." If that's you, then you'll most likely respond, "My gosh, that's me! I hurt my shoulder three years ago in an accident."

So the words I spoke in that moment from the Holy Spirit, all of a sudden you latch on to those words and you begin to connect to the Healer Himself. All I've done is initiate an encounter between you and God. You begin to connect. And once you've connected, your shoulder is made whole because He is the Healer and you can't help but be healed when you've connected with Him. It really is a simple concept.

But you may say, "Well, I connect to Him all the time. I pray to Him all the time. I'm connected to God, so what do you mean by that?"

It's important to recognize God is multifaceted, infinite in His variety of Self-expression. Maybe you connect to Him as your Provider a lot. Or maybe you've connected to Him as your heavenly Father, but perhaps you've never connected to Him as "the Healer" before.

When the Israelites came out of the desert, they'd already known that He was *Jehovah Jireh*. They'd already encountered that name of God because this revelation came about when Abraham took the ram caught in the thicket that God had provided. He said of Himself, "I will provide," and they had that history, so they knew that He was "the Provider."

But He had not revealed Himself as the Healer at that point. It wasn't until they cried out, "The water is bitter!" and God made the water sweet that He revealed to them, "I am the Lord who heals you" (Exod. 15:26). Before that time, they did not have a revelation of that name—they had not connected to that aspect of His nature before—and therefore they could not have a revelation of faith in His ability to heal them.

This is about you connecting to that aspect of God as the Healer. Sure, maybe He's always been your Provider, your Comforter, your Banner of Victory. He's been many things to you during the course of your walk with Him. But you know, when you're sick and need a healing, you need to connect with Him as the Healer. See the difference? There is a revelation of faith that comes from encountering God in one of His many facets of expression.

Back to Acts 14, here's a great example of faith operating through the inner witness. Notice it says that Paul observed this man intently. He studied him deeply for a moment, sensing what the Spirit was saying about this man. Sure enough, Paul saw the he had faith to be healed—there was no way he could have known this without a prompting inwardly from the Spirit; otherwise he'd just be guessing here.

Next, I want to point out that Paul "said with a loud voice." He wasn't whispering; he didn't use his inside voice. No, there was a boldness in the volume that Paul used when he spoke; it was a commanding utterance: "Stand up!" Notice the man leaped. I envision he was startled by Paul's "loud voice" and leaped to attention. He took it fast! Here's a guy who'd been crippled from birth—how would he even know *how* to leap? He'd never even learned to stand—the Bible says he was sitting and had never walked before.

I'm reminded of the story of Smith Wigglesworth taking a dead body and throwing it up against the wall, shouting, "Walk!" And the body did! It's a similar principle here. There was power in the words spoken, a bold courageousness that created an expectation in Paul and Wigglesworth—they expected the body to obey their command. Now, without an inward knowing that the Lord was prompting them to do so, it would just be the height of foolishness to yell at a crippled man or a corpse and tell them to walk, right? What gave these men of God that kind of confidence to speak this way? Again, their inward witness, their sensitivity to the promptings of the still, small voice.

You know, in several of Paul's letters in the New Testament, we read how he's speaking of his weakness in the flesh. The name *Paul* means "small." He speaks about his inability to do the things he wants to do in the natural (see Rom. 7). He's always speaking of himself as a bondservant, the chief of sinners, and so on (see Rom. 1:1; 1 Tim. 1:15). Yet, when Paul's in the Spirit, he's shouting at cripples, telling them to do something that in the natural is ridiculous and even rude.

Like Paul, we need to acknowledge what God is doing, and we need to acknowledge it boldly. Our words carry power, but we can't be bold in the flesh. Rather, we should be bold in the Spirit. Acts 19:11 says God worked "special miracles" through the hands of Paul (KJV). *Special* means "extraordinary." Even his hankies could be saturated with the power of God to the point of clearing out diseases and demons. Special. Shocking. Eye-opening, creative miracles that everyone could see, and it flabbergasted them. These miracles were so powerfully astounding that it actually changed the Ephesian culture. It shook the town to its roots. So, it wasn't just that someone was healed, and the people were like, "Aww, that's nice." No, they were healed in such a remarkable way, it stunned the people and blew their minds to the point that it started a riot. Isn't that special?

Paul was able to operate this way because he was emboldened by the Spirit within him and he reached out—taking it fast—expecting to see what he was feeling explosively on the inside translated just as explosively on the outside. It changed entire cities!

You too can have a revelation of faith like Paul and the man from Lystra! It is this revelation that spawns such a boldness to accelerate the operation of God's healing power in your life. Let's talk about boldness for a moment.

CHAPTER 7

MOMENTS OF BOOM!

Our Lord carried so much glory within His body that it convinced people to believe on Him and they were healed. His words carried authority to the point that it shocked the people who heard Him into an ecstatic state (see Luke 4:32). As the Anointed One of God operating as a Man, He initiated an encounter between the Father and the people who heard His bold words that created the healings.

We don't see Jesus praying for people with a meek, whispering voice. How many times have you prayed with someone, "Jesus, please touch them," in a kind of quiet, hesitant voice? I can't be the only one who's done this. "Ooh. Well. Maybe I feel a little twinge of the anointing here. Well, that's good. Just bless them, Jesus." And the person, maybe they receive a marginal improvement, and thank God for that—but there's no *ta-dah!* climax, no *punctuation* to the encounter, an exclamation point where the person *knows* they encountered God.

Jesus didn't leave people that way, wondering, "Well, *maybe* I met with God. I mean, I kinda feel a little tingly." No, when He laid hands on them, *boom!* They knew they'd just had an encounter with the Almighty.

It's important for us to feel those moments of *boom!* and acknowledge them. I know that a lot of healing is internal, so it's not always, "Look at me! I can walk!" But there needs to be an undeniable moment when both people have acknowledged there was an impartation of healing virtue. Even if the healing itself doesn't manifest on the spot, that person who was being ministered to walks away *knowing* they just met with God. We as the person ministering to them need to *know* that virtue went out from our spirits by the Holy Spirit, into theirs. Jesus was able to perceive this—so should we (see Mark 5:30; Luke 8:46).

It is important to feel those moments and acknowledge them; and when they acknowledge them, even if the full manifestation isn't there, they know they've received healing virtue into their body and there's a quickening work of the Lord occurring.

When Jesus spoke to the fig tree, "Nobody will eat fruit from you again," there was absolutely no visible change to the tree when He said that (see Mark 11). But the thing was dead, right? It was done at that moment; the roots died. But it wasn't till the next day that the disciples were able to see the tree withered.

How much more so with words of life, when we speak a miracle of recreation into something? Hey, I like it when it manifests instantly; who doesn't? But sometimes people come and receive an impartation, and the miracle isn't instantaneous—there is a distinct difference between "workings of miracles" and "gifts of healing." One is an immediate occurrence, an action visible in the physical realm instantaneously. "My arm grew out in front of everyone's eyes." The other is a process over time, a recovery toward health.

"My diabetes was cured over the weekend." Both are supernatural because God is the Source of healing and miracles, but it is the Spirit who chooses how to operate in which way.

We are commanded to lay hands on the sick, and the Bible says they shall recover. That's our role to play. And, yes, we are all striving for the instant miracles, and I believe we are seeing more and more of this type of manifestation. But let us not neglect the equally important gifts of healing.

The person you lay hands on, if he or she receives that impartation of healing virtue, then they *are* healed. No ifs, ands, or buts. You just tell them to grab hold of that virtue and watch what God does. His healing power *is* moving—the substance of His anointing *is* there. This is a fact because the Bible declares it as fact.

Hebrews 11:1 teach that faith is a substance; that means it's a tangible thing, real and true at the moment someone speaks a word of faith and believes that word will do what God says it will do. That substance materializes exactly when the word of faith is believed by the person who is being prayed for. Everything necessary to complete the healing or miracle is there. The manifestation will start to occur at that point of contact with both parties believing the word of faith spoken—the minister believes that he or she is speaking a word in faith; the person being ministered to receives that word in faith. Therefore, it is so important that we *speak* forth that word of faith in boldness—quite literally, a moment of boom!

Let me share with you a story of an MRI of a woman's back, and if any of you reading this have a misalignment in any way—in your spine, or an arm or a leg is too short—take it fast!

When I say MRI, I mean it was a Holy Spirit-led MRI. That's not to be trite. It was like a play-by-play of what God was doing in this woman with the crooked spine. She stood before us, and it's like we could just see what the Lord was doing in the spiritual realm, just like an MRI on the screen. It was simply a matter of announcing what God was doing as He was showing us—and, of course, the importance of her receiving what God was doing almost instantaneously—healing her as we described what we saw.

We could see in the spiritual realm the Lord touching the top of her spine. And then the anointing started coming down, so we would just describe the image from God. Coupled with this was the inner witness and the still, small voice, working in tandem.

I share this to show that these "moments of boom" are actually orchestrated by the same Spirit, but He is using several means all at the same time to convey what was happening to this woman. I believe that we need to be open and cultivate a sensitivity to the Spirit who moves in a multifaceted manner. Often we focus on one particular type of manifestation, perhaps to the exclusion of others, and it *could* be a hindrance to what God is wanting to do. I don't think healing is really an either/or situation; rather, it is embracing *all* that God is doing, utilizing all of our spiritual faculties, so to speak, in order to place ourselves in a position to be used by Him.

As we described what we were seeing and sensing, it was like we heard, "I am straightening her back." So we declared, "He is straightening your back. Do you feel that?"

And the woman described a burning sensation going on in her back. This continued until she was totally set free, praise God! It's the same thing for you—if you are in need of healing, realize God *is* moving in many different ways—but your healing is here; take Him fast!

Now here's a good place for a quick aside. For those who are ministering to others for healing, you don't have to say they "got healed"—it's not a matter of claiming it till it happens, like "fake it until you make it." It's alright to use language like, "You've been touched by God," when you sense healing virtue going into them.

I'm not disregarding the way healing has been administered in the past. I mean if you don't *know* that the virtue has gone into the person, keep praying. It's okay to ask the person, "How are you feeling? Ten percent better; fifty percent better?" It is not wrong to proceed in the ways we were taught; it's okay to use a "method" when praying for healing.

I'm just saying let's add to it as the Holy Spirit directs, as we all grow in the Lord—and we all need to grow; none of us has attained perfection when it comes to healing and miracles! Be open to the Spirit and don't rely on tradition, especially when it comes to healing. Like Isaiah 43:19 says, God is doing a new thing!

Even compared to a few months ago, it's not the same for me when I pray for people—I've grown a little bolder in proclaiming the freedom of the Lord in their lives. I had a stunning realization of just how important it is to declare these "events" in healing when I minister to someone.

Really, how often did Jesus ask someone, "Are you healed?" We know He did with the blind man, but most often Jesus was just telling *them* they were healed. We all want to minister as Jesus did, and I think it's important that we start stepping out into that deeper level of declaring what *has* happened rather than asking for something *to* happen. We need to believe these moments of boom are here, right now, waiting to be activated by our revelation of faith. It's just a different mindset, and one that I think the Spirit is imparting into His people in this time of accelerated healing.

CHAPTER 8

THE CONVICTION OF FAITH

The second level of faith is *conviction*. You have a personal conviction, just like the man in Acts 14. He was there, and he had a conviction. You see this in the Gospels all the time. I try to look at all the miracles of Jesus and how they happened; what were the circumstances surrounding the healing? Of course there are so many; it would take a lifetime to fully grasp each one, and so many of them aren't even recorded! What we know of the life of Jesus as recorded in the Gospels is just a small fraction of the miracles He performed. The Bible says if all of them were recorded, the world couldn't contain all the books written about them (see John 21:25). I love that! I wish I could've been there to see all of them, but hey, we're seeing them all now, right? Jesus promised us these "greater works" and I, for one, can't wait to be a witness! I am convinced we are living in one of the most exciting times of human history!

Anyway, personal conviction, the second step, is directly tied to the third level of faith—*action* to do something about your conviction. There needs to be a corresponding action to what you are convinced of inside. Paul told the man, "Stand up on your feet!" The crippled man still needed to stand upon on his feet. This was putting his inward personal conviction to outward visible action.

There must be action. The woman with the issue of blood knew the importance of taking action in response to faith. "If I just touch the hem of His garment." To the lepers Jesus said, "Go and show yourself to the priest." There was a required action there.

I've been reading First and Second Kings a lot lately, and it's funny, because I've noticed that with Elijah and Elisha there was almost always an associated action that went with every miraculous expression they were believing for. Seems to me this is a principle in God's Word.

Remember in 2 Kings 6 the story of the floating axe head? Here they are, chopping wood, and the man loses a borrowed axe head. "What are we gonna do?" And here's Elisha: "Where'd it happen?" They point, and he throws a piece of wood in the water, which causes the axe head to float to the surface. What a strange and powerful miracle!

Or how about right before this story, in 2 Kings 4, the poisonous pot of stew? What does Elisha do to purify it? Nothing more than throw some flour in it.

It's funny how, with God, we do the small, little, possible part. That's all God is asking from us—just a tiny, little possible, and He does the amazingly impossible. It's such a small part we do. Sometimes just showing up at a meeting is enough! This is God working with us (see Mark 16:20); it's His idea of what it means to co-labor. It isn't a 50/50 situation where we do half and God does half. No, it's more like we do .000001 percent, and He does the rest. That's why He gets all the glory!

Because it's 99.9 percent Him and we're doing such a small part, we should never get puffed up. Yes, our part is important, don't misunderstand, but it's nearly *all* Him. We have no right to touch God's glory. Sometimes, our greatest "part" in co-laboring with Him is simply to cultivate such a level of humility that we get out of the way, so to speak, and let Him move. Humility is a huge part of accelerated healing.

Many times it's simply an act of obedience that is our part in the release. It can be something as simple as just showing up to the meeting with an expectation to receive. It's like God is saying, "Okay, that's enough; you showed up here. You must have some faith, or you wouldn't be here, right?"

Just a little something—that's all He's asking. In the Bible, people came to Jesus with all different levels of faith, and God healed them all the same. Just don't come with *nothing*, dear reader—come with something, just a little part, and He will do the rest.

That's why we often say to people receiving healing, "Do something that you couldn't do before. Test it out." You know, I've found that very often it's when someone is testing it out that they start to get healed. Now, sure, they might not be healed all at once; it can be a process. So that's why I'll often say to them, "Hey, if you're feeling at least eighty percent better, wave your arms at me." Sometimes that's all it takes for the other 20 percent.

In many cases you receive healing virtue into your body, and it takes a while for you to be completely made whole. It often doesn't happen all at once. That doesn't make it any less supernatural.

I've learned in meetings that when I said, "If you're one hundred percent healed, let us know," people would be hesitant because they're still in the process of receiving their healing. I've learned to ask instead, "If you feel God's doing something…." This is an opportunity for the person receiving healing to acknowledge God moving in their body.

Remember, *acknowledging what He's doing is a key to getting increase and sustaining your healing.*

A few years ago, we prayed for a man, and he got healed—I think it was his shoulder. But I said to him, "Now look, if the pain tries to come back on you, just laugh at it. Don't receive it back, okay? Remember this moment that you were healed. Remember what happened here."

I asked him, "Are you healed right now?"

"Yeah."

"Raise your arm. Do you have any pain?"

"No."

"So you know God has done something to you."

"Yes, He did."

"Okay. Well, stand on what you just told me, because that's truth. You're telling me you're better; something happened, and you're healed—remember this is what God did for you in this moment. Don't let it get stolen from you, okay?"

This dialogue may seem redundant, unimportant. But I think it's very important to confirm this with the people I minister to because often, if the pain or illness tries to come back, they'll say, "Oh, maybe I wasn't healed." They'll start to deny what they know happened in that moment of encounter with Jesus, and the thing will start to come back on them.

I hate it when people don't retain their healing because they don't stand on what has taken place. Laughing in the face of your "returning symptoms" *is* taking God fast! Don't fall for the lie that God didn't touch you!

Three days later that man who was healed was sharing his testimony. He said, "Yeah my shoulder got healed, but it was a funny thing—the next day I was in the shower, and all of a sudden the pain started to come back. But I remember what that guy told me, if the pain comes back, just laugh at it. So I did. And when I laughed at it, the pain left completely and has not returned since."

Praise God!

Remember. Remember. Remember. You know, part of the reason why the Israelites had such a hard time is they *forgot*. They didn't stand on the things that the Lord had already done for them and who He was, His nature and character that is unchanging. They didn't stand on the history they had with Him. The longer you're in this with God, the more history you develop.

CHAPTER 9

HISTORICAL SIGNIFICANCE

My wife's been healed of other things besides her knee. She was hypoglycemic, and the Lord corrected that. I mean, it's like God just loves to heal her. Whenever something new creeps up, she just gets healed. Praise the Lord, she knows she's loved by God—she's experienced it firsthand, and it's shaped the course of her life (and mine).

You, too, have a history in the Lord in many different things. It is important to stand and remember those things. That's a component of accelerated healing, because you stand in confidence, knowing that what God has done in the past He will do again in your present.

> *For I am the Lord, I do not change* (Malachi 3:6).

This is an eternal truth—what the Lord has done in the past, based on His character and nature, He will always do throughout all of eternity. One hundred billion years from now He will still be Healer. He can't change that aspect of His existence.

Like so many couples just starting out, my wife and I had no money when we got married. We moved to Baton Rouge, Louisiana, based on a call of God we felt was on our lives. Janet and I were Spirit-filled in 1996. We call Him the "Holy Ghost." Some places, He's the Holy Spirit, but back then we said, "We got the Holy Ghost." That's a great expression. "I got the Holy Ghost!"

Janet "got the Holy Ghost" two weeks before me. That's because she's more spiritual than I am. Typical. Had to figure that would happen, right? So I'd be provoked to jealousy. Janet's got the Holy Ghost now, so I gotta press in.

Anyway, I got the Holy Ghost two weeks after she did, and it was an awesome experience; but it was still painfully obvious, even after heeding the Lord's call to move to Cajun country and pressing into this baptism in the Spirit, we still had *no money* at all. I mean, no money. And we wanted to start a small group. Our church called them "touch groups," which sounds like a silly name; I'm glad they changed it. Really, it was a prayer group.

But we needed a place to meet with our "touch group." I mean, we didn't even have a couch or anything, and we wanted to start a small group. Just young and broke.

I remember telling her, "God's gonna give us a couch, honey." Janet nodded. "That's right. God's gonna give us a couch."

We were young and had newly "got the Holy Ghost," so we just believed it. Sure enough, a couple days later, there's a knock on the front door, and there's this guy standing there.

"You want a couch?"

We had never seen this guy before, had no idea who he was; he didn't even know I needed a couch. That's the kind of crazy stuff that God does.

My point here is history in the Lord. We have a history now. And I'm confident you have had the Lord do something similar in your past—if you've been born again any length of time, God *has* done something for you.

That moment established for us a history of Him being *Jehovah Jireh*. We always have that couch moment. If something happens and we hit something difficult, it's no problem. Janet and I just tell each other, "Remember the couch? Remember what God did there? Remember?"

You need to remember—always remember your history in the Lord so that it never gets stolen from you. Remember it, appreciate it, treasure it. And when you see someone else get healed, rejoice for them and remember it as part of your history, that you viewed their moment of encounter—and God is equally available to all. What He did for them, He will do for you.

It's really a "posture" that you take standing in the Lord. Posture is super important when it comes to healing ministry. You could have poor posture, slouching and stoop-shouldered: "Well, God healed them, but I know they're in sin. I know what they're up to, and God healed them. Why doesn't He heal me?" That's poor posture.

Or you could have correct posture—throw your shoulders back, suck in your gut, stand straight and tall: "God, thank You; You're such a good Father. You healed them out of Your goodness, and thank You, Lord, I know You're going to heal me. I appreciate You so much!"

That's the kind of posture to step into a healing, right there. The other one's clearly not. That's not where you want to be to see accelerated healing! So much of receiving healing is about our heart posture, our heart attitude.

And it's the testimony of Jesus. I love Revelation 19:10: "And I fell at his feet to worship him. But he said to me, 'See that you do not do that! I am your fellow servant, and of your brethren who have the testimony of Jesus. Worship God! For the testimony of Jesus is the spirit of prophecy.'"

I'm sure this verse will pop up throughout the book. The testimony of Jesus is the spirit of prophecy. What does that mean? It means that the very thing. Say someone gets a healing in their body—that healing is a testimony of what Jesus did in their body. The testimony of that healing could become a prophetic word for someone else to step into *their* healing. It's prophetic; like, "That happened for them, it's gonna happen for you, too, if you receive that testimony of what Jesus did."

That's why testimonies are so powerful—it is the prophetic Spirit of Jesus in operation. Wherever I minister, I always share testimony of what I've seen the Lord do; it raises the corporate level of faith tremendously. People begin to realize it's not as hard as they think to receive healing. In fact, it's actually easy when you become convinced that a) He loves you with the same fervency He loves His Son; and b) He's there, the power and presence of God is there for signs, wonders, and miraculous, creative miracles of healing. It's all there for us because He loves us.

> *But without faith it is impossible to please Him, for he who comes to God must believe that He is, and that He is a rewarder of those who diligently seek Him* (Hebrews 11:6).

We have seen so many people healed based on the testimony of other people's healings. I learned this principle from Randy Clark. He'll just show videos of people getting healed, and people will get healed watching the videos of people getting healed.

I remember a man who was totally blind in one eye, watching one of these videos, and his eye completely, instantly opened up just from watching the video, and he started connecting to God based on seeing these testimonies. This is just like the crippled man in Acts 14; Paul's speaking, the guy's hearing him speak, he begins to connect to God based on what he's hearing, and he gets healed. It's the same principle at play here in watching the videos.

I believe it's the same as the woman with the issue of blood. I love this woman, don't you? I can't wait to meet her in heaven; she's one of my heroes. She obviously had heard that this Man, Jesus, could heal, and just based on that testimony, she convinced herself that if she could just touch the tip of His clothes, she would be healed as well. She wouldn't allow anything to stop her from receiving her miracle. She didn't get "talked out of it," you know? She heard of what Jesus had done in recent history and expected the same manifestation of grace and power in her life.

CHAPTER 10

TAKE IT BY FORCE

Jesus tells us in Matthew 11:12, "And from the days of John the Baptist until now the kingdom of heaven suffers violence, and the violent take it by force."

I like that verse. It contains so much revelation regarding how we should posture our heart and the resolve we must have that it is worth taking the time to expound further on what was introduced in chapter 3. Once again, it doesn't mean you're forceful with the Kingdom. It means you're forceful against the things that are *keeping* you from the Kingdom.

The woman with the issue of blood was not forceful with Jesus at all, but she was forceful against the powers that were keeping her from Jesus. We know according to Jewish law she shouldn't have been touching Him. She shouldn't have been around those people at all. She shouldn't have been pushing her way through. There are a lot of things she shouldn't have done according to the world's standards, but she ignored all of that and pushed through the world to receive her healing from Jesus.

> *And suddenly, a woman who had a flow of blood for twelve years came from behind and touched the hem of His garment. For she said to herself, "If only I may touch His garment, I shall be made well"* (Matthew 9:20-21).

I love this confession; it's just so good. She said to herself, "Self, I know if I can just make it to the bottom of His cloak, I'll be healed." Powerful! Full of faith. That's why she's honored in the Bible for all eternity.

> *But Jesus turned around, and when He saw her He said, "Be of good cheer, daughter; your faith has made you well." And the woman was made well from that hour* (Matthew 9:22).

First, there was the *revelation* based on what she knew about Jesus—most likely from others' testimonies or seeing Him heal others with her own eyes. Second, there came a personal *conviction* that Jesus could heal her. Third, there was *action* behind her conviction. "If I could just touch His cloak." This is speaking of the conviction in her heart.

> *A good man out of the good treasure of his heart brings forth good; and an evil man out of the evil treasure of his heart brings forth evil. For out of the abundance of the heart his mouth speaks* (Luke 6:45).

We could phrase it, "Out of the conviction of the heart the mouth speaks."

"I will be healed," she said. And Jesus' response was exactly what she was expecting. "Take heart, your faith has healed you!"

Now let's tie this woman's victory to the principle of the testimony of Jesus being the spirit of prophecy. (Again, Revelation 19:10.) If we just jump ahead five chapters from the testimony in Matthew 9, we'll see something amazing.

> *And when the men of that place recognized Him, they sent out into all that surrounding region, brought to Him all who were sick, and begged Him that they might only touch the hem of His garment. And as many as touched it were made perfectly well* (Matthew 14:35-36).

It was the woman first, right? Did you notice that? (That'll preach.) But see, now it's the men jumping on the garment-hem bandwagon. The first recorded place of anybody touching the hem of His garment was the woman with the issue of blood. But now when the men of another region see Jesus, they ask to do the same thing. I wonder where they got the idea from?

See how that woman's faith to do what she did opened up the healing for all those other people? Because of the faith of one woman, many, many more people were healed. That's the multiplication of the Kingdom—that is the testimony of Jesus being ratified by the Spirit of prophecy. That is why the Kingdom of heaven "suffers violence." People are taking God fast, by force—that's accelerated healing.

That's why Jesus says the Kingdom is like a little mustard seed. It starts out like this, but its growth curve is explosively exponential. Faith is contagious. Once one person gets a hold of it, it quickly spreads to others—a vast multiplication that takes place.

When I share the testimony of my wife's knee getting healed and people lay hold of that, their knees get healed as well. Based on my wife's testimony, we've seen hundreds of knees get healed. That's acceleration. Because of one word of knowledge a man received nearly a decade ago, hundreds of knees have been healed. Isn't that amazing?

The Kingdom just blows me away. It's so big, I can't grasp it—I just enjoy it. I'm only along for the ride. I don't know how He does what He does; it's a mystery to me, but I like being a part of it. I'm having a whole lot of fun, and my wife has a lot of grace for me to travel and be on the road, because she said if Bill Johnson hadn't gone on that trip, if *his* wife hadn't released him, Janet's knee wouldn't have gotten healed.

"If you don't go," she tells me, "then how are those people going to get healed? How is all this going to get multiplied?" That's why I'm writing this book—I want to see that multiplication of the Kingdom as you take it by force.

Maybe you're reading this and you need a healing. Here's what I want you to do, based on this testimony alone—do you believe what I'm sharing about my wife's healing? Then I want you to stand, right where you're reading this, if you've got some kind of joint problem—an ankle, a knee, a foot, a hip. Go ahead and stand, put your conviction into action based on this revelation.

> *Lord, I thank You for every person who is reading this right now in faith. I thank You for the testimony of healing Janet, and based on that testimony, let it be a prophetic word now for everyone standing, believing You will do the same thing for them. I speak a miracle of recreation now, and I thank You for Your power to be able to speak that forth.*

Now I want you, dear reader, to act out your personal conviction that caused you to stand in the first place. Don't hesitate—take Him fast! Do something you couldn't do before with that joint, or whatever was wrong, and watch what God does in this moment, right now, as you read this in faith. Watch how God mends bones that were crooked, stitches fibers back together that were torn asunder, and reconnects nerves instantaneously.

Is that happening for you? Is it eighty percent better? Keep standing in faith. It *will* come. Thank You, God!

Now when your full healing manifests, you will have a lot of faith to see other people healed from the same thing. Your testimony is powerful because it is full of faith as there is no doubt or unbelief in your own healing. Does that make sense? Make yourself available—I'm sure you know someone who needs healing. We all do. Pray a real simple prayer with them, multiply the Kingdom—accelerate that healing!

You know, Jesus' prayers were very simple. That's what I love about Him—He's so simple in many ways. I thank God for His simplicity!

Let's take this a step further. Janet's testimony can be used to encourage your faith for any type of healing. It's all the same to God. Perhaps you're reading this right now and have breathing issues. Maybe a deviated septum, asthma, polyps—in the lungs, in the nose. Maybe you even have cancer. If you're reading this now, I encourage you to go ahead and stand up.

> *I thank You, Jesus, for honoring Your testimony as Healer—thank You for touching these dear readers and loving them just as You love me. We just speak for those breathing issues to be obliterated now—every lung open, every nose open.*

Now take a deep breath as your act of faith. Do something that you couldn't do before.

What about people with eye problems? Again, it's all the same where God is concerned. Cataracts? Eye deterioration? Maybe even blindness, and someone is reading this to you right now. I want you to stand up. Let's just say a simple prayer together aloud: "Cataracts, floaters, whatever—dissolve right now in the name of Jesus. Blind eyes, be opened!"

Now test it out.

God is so good. Just keep giving Him praise, thanksgiving—these are keys to unlocking the accelerated healing of God, stepping into more. I've seen that so many times where someone will start to feel the presence of God and they get healed as a byproduct of simply worshiping Him.

You can see it when someone starts to step in with the right posture. If they're saying, "Yeah, I see this, but it still hurts." *That's* not the right posture.

"Wow, He did *that*. If He's done that, I know He will do *this*." That's the right posture. That's the key to releasing more. You start thanking Him for what He's done, and you get more. You start questioning why He's not doing more, and you get less.

CHAPTER 11

THIS TIME IT'S PERSONAL!

The gift of faith is yours because the Spirit is yours (see John 4:16; Eph. 1:13; 4:30; 2 Cor. 1:22). It is only *one* gift—the Spirit Himself (see 1 Cor. 12:4). And when we need faith, it is already ours because we already have the Spirit inside us. I hear people always asking God for "more faith"—I understand their intentions, but in reality that's an errant concept. Romans 12:3 says that God has *already* dealt to everyone the "measure of faith." That is because He has already poured out His Spirit (see Acts 2:17). You don't really need *more* faith; you need to use the faith you already have by quickly acting upon this revelation. Yes, faith needs to be fed (see Rom. 10:17), but really what we are doing is making the faith already present effectual (see Philem. 6; Jude 20). We could say our faith needs to be quickened by the Spirit. (See Romans 8:11 KJV—*quicken* means made alive, made active.)

Because the testimony of Jesus is the spirit of prophecy, let me intersperse some testimonies here in an effort to give opportunity for the Spirit to quicken your faith. This isn't to build us up as ministers; rather, it's to build up the faith that you have, thereby making it effectual for your healing.

We had a man come up into the prayer line with no hamstring in one of his legs. I'm not sure *where* the hamstring went; I didn't ask. But you know, a hamstring is pretty important, right? I don't really know how a person could walk without one. In any case, this man didn't have one. A gift of faith arose, we felt the tangible presence of God, and I said simply, "I see this surge happening right now. God is doing something in you right this moment. Begin to feel where that hamstring is supposed to be." Wham! This hamstring just went down his leg! We all kind of jumped in shock because it was such an instant thing. Of course, the man starts running around, going crazy, praising God! Absolutely wild to see something like that.

But here's the deal. Are you missing something in your body as you read this? Cartilage? A whole body part? Then I want you to pounce, take Him fast! Don't hesitate! I believe the Lord wants you just as miraculously made whole as that man. Same God, same power residing in you, me and that man. Take it by force!

I remember another instance—there was a word of knowledge, and this lady came up saying, "I'm allergic to fruit. I haven't been able to eat any fruit in years." Well, God touched her, and she went and scarfed down a whole pineapple. Her husband was on staff at the church, and he was cracking up because he didn't warn her that eating a whole acidic pineapple in one sitting is a pretty sure way to hurt your tongue. (And probably a tummy ache after, but I'm sure it was worth it.)

Okay, so are you allergic to something? Do you have digestive issues? Again, the God who touched that woman is the same God residing in your born-again spirit. Take Him fast! The same blood that ratified the New Covenant two millennia ago is operating in your "today" to bring healing to you. It's not something He wants to do; it's something He's already done. Take it by force!

When we read of the healings Jesus did while on this earth, it seems no two were *exactly* alike—they all seem customized, don't they? One time He's spitting on the ground and making mud packs, telling a man blind from birth to go wash in the pool of Siloam (see John 9). Another time He's sticking His fingers in a person's ears, commanding them to "Be opened!" (see Mark 7). Another time He's grabbing a dead child by the hand and telling her, "Little girl, arise" (see Luke 8).

Why is it that each person receives from the Lord in a slightly different way? The answer is we each have a unique and personal God who is connecting with His unique person He created. If God bothered to make each person on the planet with unique fingerprints, doesn't it stand to reason that He wants to connect uniquely with each of us?

It is important to remember that divine healing is personal. There is no magic formula that works for all of us the exact same way. Yes, there are biblical principles that apply to all of us, but when it comes to receiving directly from the Lord it is unique to each person who comes to Him. The way God operates in my life may not be exactly identical to how He operates in yours, but the result is the same—we are healed. *How* God chooses to bring about that healing may vary from person to person. I think it's important we don't get into a "cookie cutter" mentality concerning the *how*. Rather, I believe we always need to be focused on the *who*—the individual person with a healing need. We need to have a revelation of *who* we are in Christ.

Jesus' healing miracles are all quite different in the Word, proving this point. Sometimes He laid hands on the person; sometimes

He just spoke to them; other times, He made mud and smeared it on their eyes, telling them to go wash it off. And they weren't healed until they were obedient and washed.

We serve an infinitely unique God! *Our role as sons and daughters ministering healing in His name is all about connecting the person to God.* If they can touch God, they *will* get healed, because He *is* Healer. We are simply helping *them* initiate an encounter with *Him*, because when a person encounters Him as Healer they are healed. There is no other outcome when one meets with God, because He is the God who heals. It is not simply a power He possesses, it is an attribute of His very makeup and existence. There is healing because there is God. So when one meets with God, one is healed.

This is how the gifts of the Spirit help us to connect that person to the Lord. If we receive a word of knowledge revealing a particular condition in someone, that establishes a connection between them and God. So one of the primary purposes of the gifts, therefore, is to create a divine encounter in someone else's life.

CHAPTER 12

WE'RE DEAD

Praise is another way we can personally connect to God. As simple as it sounds, it is the atmosphere of praise and worship that instigates a physical manifestation of His glory, and, again, making a connection with Him creates the environment where healing comes. His glory is the manifestation of His awesome, mighty worth and "weightiness," and because He *is* healing (it is an element or byproduct of His existence, not just something He can perform) His manifested glory cannot help *but* heal. Praise establishes the atmosphere for His glory to be tangibly perceived in our bodies, and when someone is connected to God, they are healed. The atmosphere of praise creates an atmosphere of glory, and when His presence is established people have an encounter with Him and are healed as a result.

In Los Angeles, at the Azusa Street revival of the early 1900s, it seemed at times, when the glory was thick, it didn't matter who prayed, how they prayed, or what the condition was—the person got healed simply because of the atmosphere of praise that established the tangible presence of Almighty God. In other words, the encounter was initiated by God's glory and presence.

Healing happens in a number of different ways. Perhaps someone receives their healing just walking up to the prayer line as an act of faith. Sometimes a person needs to be prayed for, and sometimes they're healed just sitting in their seats as they worship Him silently. It is *always* personal and oftentimes *personalized* for the individual. God is many-faceted and operates in a variety of ways. The point is to make a connection with God in some way, and the healing will be the result of that connection. Again, we reach a point where we take Him fast!

Sometimes that is all a person needs to connect to God and get healed; others maybe need a word of knowledge or someone to pray for them. Words of knowledge connect people to God and make them aware that He is healing now. In our healing meetings, we see all of that going on. Some people just walk in and are healed; others get prayed for first, then they are healed. It's different for each person.

Sometimes God heals sovereignly, just a representation of His glory, but more often than not we must make a connection to Him in order to receive His personal attributes (healing, in this case) in our lives. We know that people approached Jesus on this earth with varying degrees of faith, hope, and understanding. The Lord always met them where they were to initiate an encounter with the Father. But there wasn't some blanket requisite where their faith had to be sitting at an 8.75 to a 9.5 before God healed them. It isn't some magical formula—it is about connecting with God on a personal level.

You know, I don't think Lazarus had a whole lot of faith, right? He was dead. Nevertheless, Jesus made a personal connection with the Father that resulted in a corpse coming out of a tomb! (See John 11:41-43.) The Lord used His friend's death as a means of making a connection between the people and the Father. This is why He asked Martha, "Do you believe this?" (John 11:26). Jesus worked with each person at their level of faith to make a connection between them and His Father.

An example on the other side of the spectrum is the centurion in Matthew 8. This man had tapped into a whole other level, I believe, receiving a divine revelation of the authority that resided in Jesus based upon his understanding of his own authority. This was such a unique occurrence that the Bible says Jesus marveled (see Matt. 8:10). A Roman was able to make that kind of connection to the Hebrew God for his servant's healing.

So people came to the Lord with differing levels of faith, and yet the result was the same—He healed them. Some had very little faith: "If You can do anything, have compassion" (Mark 9:22), all the way to extreme faith: "Just say the word and my servant will be healed," or, "If I just touch the hem of His garment, I will be healed."

Even if they had next to no faith, it was enough for Jesus to work with, and He healed them *all*. Yet many times, as in the case of the centurion, people recognized Jesus's ability even before it had been demonstrated. This opened up a realm of faith before they had witnessed His healing power in action.

So these examples of healing are not so much about *how* but about *who*! The woman with the issue of blood believed she would be healed because of *who* she was touching. The centurion believed his servant would be healed if it was *Jesus* who said the words.

The important point to take away from all this is, we need to make sure we don't focus on *how* someone will get healed—*how* to pray for them to see the desired result—rather, we need to focus on *who* He is, where He is, being led by *Him* to the desired result.

I know that we all want the "how to's." (How do I pray for the sick? How do I see creative miracles happen?) That's not necessarily *wrong*—I hope this book is giving you some of those how to's. It's fine to start there, but our heart's desire should be to then let God show you some personal elements of His healing grace. Then the *how to*'s are changed into *His to*'s. It becomes more and more about *who* is healing than *how* He is healing.

No matter where your personal level of faith sits—if you're just starting out at a "Lazarus level" or if you're somewhere in the middle like the father with the epileptic son in Mark 9, or if you're at the centurion's level—it is very important to remember the truth of Galatians 2:20: "I have been crucified with Christ; it is no longer I who live, but Christ lives in me; and the life which I now live in the flesh I live by faith in the Son of God, who loved me and gave Himself for me."

Think about that for a second. I died. It's no longer me living, but rather Christ living in me. I am not "just John." John's dead, and good riddance because John was pretty lousy at just about everything. But with Christ living in me, suddenly those limitations of "just John" have been tossed out the window. I am a new being; it's a fusion with Christ inside me. We're one just as God the Father and God the Son are One. This was Jesus' prayer in John 17. So I am "we" now—Christ living inside me, as one, through His gift of salvation. That's the ultimate personal connection, isn't it?

This life we live by faith, and this is a gift from Christ, so our whole life—in a certain sense—is a gift of faith.

It makes me feel so good when I pray, "*We (Christ in me)* speak a miracle of recreation." Boy, that takes the pressure off "just John." And what's even better is Christ in me manifests Himself differently from Christ in you. Each of us with our own unique expression and gifting—it's a truly beautiful thing.

Ministering becomes a lot easier when it is *Christ in you*. When you minister as who you really are—Christ in you—then nothing is impossible!

We need to constantly remind ourselves that we are not "just ourselves" but rather Christ within us. In Him, you and He are one, just as He is One with the Father. Just as we took Him *now* for salvation and became one with Him in the new birth, we must take Him *now* as the One living inside us who brings about the healing. Even though God is One, He co-labors with the Son and, in turn, co-labors with us.

When you became born again, your life was not your own—it doesn't belong to you, it belongs to God. You're dead, and the only reason you're alive is because Christ is living within you. So therefore, He wants His habitation spic and span. Take Him now!

I used to say foolish things when I'd see God move through me. (I'm sure I still do, but hopefully I'm growing.) "That's not me," I'd say. "That's God!" Okay, yes, we *all* know it *is* God doing the work, of course—in myself, I can't heal a gnat with a tummy ache, come on. But saying those things creates a separation between the person and Christ within them. Really, it can be a form of false humility. I don't think God ever intended there to be that kind of separation. It is Christ *in* me that is the hope of glory (see Col. 1:27). Working together, Him *in* you, out *through* you, to affect the changes people need in their lives. *We* are co-laborers with God Almighty.

This whole process of accelerated healing is about learning to flow in Him as sons (and daughters) of God. We flow in Him by honoring Him and by faith taking Him at His Word. Just as we must take it by faith that we are new creations and Christ's Spirit is now living within us, similarly we must take it by faith that God is as good as His Word concerning His promises of physical healing.

CHAPTER 13

CULTIVATING SENSITIVITY

Most likely you've heard faith messages on "don't focus on your problems," and that's really true. If we focus on our problems, we're in trouble. But I remember a gentleman who had metal down his spine, and we laid hands on him for healing. The presence of the Lord was tangible, and as we focused on worshiping the Healer, standing there under His glory, I came to understand that we shouldn't focus on what needs to happen ("he needs a new back") any more than focus on the problem (the metal). As if, somehow, God wasn't aware that was why he was standing in the prayer line to begin with.

Rather, we needed to remain focused only on the Healer Himself. God knew what the man needed, so we weren't trying to "get Him" to do anything by talking about the problem or the solution.

Instead, we stood there worshiping God, following the rhythms of the Spirit, until there was a connection—in this case, a tangible flow of heat. Once that heat built to a surge, we knew he had been touched by God, and sure enough he was completely set free, running around the church, bending and stretching and moving as he never had been able to with the metal before! Praise God!

I'm not saying we're never supposed to speak to the situation and command a change. My point is, our sole focus needs to be Jesus as the Healer—and if the Spirit directs us to speak to the solution or the problem, then fine. But often, I find we're trying to "convince" God of a solution to a need in our lives, as if He were unaware of it. (That's really kind of silly when you think about it. "Oh, Lord, don't You know what I'm going through?") Again, this separates us—making each person an individual with God needing to come to us from the outside to fix a problem, rather than allowing Him to work *in* us by just taking our energy and focus and directing it on Him alone.

I remember in Kansas a man came for prayer who had a plastic shoulder. I didn't know they really put *plastic* in people; I thought "plastic surgery" was just a phrase, but his shoulder was plastic and he hardly had any range of motion at all. Again, we waited upon the Lord, worshiping Him, thanking Him, focusing on Him as the Healer.

Often after a time, there is a surge of healing virtue that goes into a person standing there for prayer, and that happened in this case. It was powerful! The man was so excited, we knew *something* had happened to him. There was a medical doctor at the meeting, which was great because she was able to testify: "I know plastic, and this *isn't* plastic; this is bone!" God had replaced the plastic shoulder with a real one, and the man could move it just like normal. Isn't God good?

Listen, if you have metal or ceramic or plastic or whatever—some foreign substance in your body that needs to be dissolved—*take Him fast!* Don't hesitate. Accelerated healing comes from an understanding that God is working *in* us to change us outwardly, and He is *more* than knowledgeable concerning what needs to happen! (See Matthew 6:8.) Focus on Him, not what you want to have happen.

When you step into the awareness of Christ in you, it activates the inner witness. When you step into the awareness that it is "we"—not you and Christ separately, but you *and* Christ working together—it changes how you approach healing. Tapping into the inner witness is so important in terms of healing because it is your spirit, by *the* Spirit, showing you what God is doing through you.

I know we all want the grandiose *boom!* Step into open visions! And that is important, but all of that type of explosive manifestation starts as an inward knowing or leading of the Spirit within you. So if that isn't cultivated and deepened, how can we expect the outward visions and the like?

I'd say more than ninety percent of healing and, really, any work of the Spirit in our lives is perceived by the inner witness. It is only by honoring the Spirit's presence in our lives, taking time to focus on Him *in* us, that we can deepen that inward knowing. We cannot underestimate the importance of the still, small voice (see 1 Kings 19:12).

There is a slight difference between the inward knowing and the still, small voice—though really, it's all just the Spirit working through us. The inward knowing is almost a "yes or no" kind of nudging or prompting in your spirit—you just know that you know something. Hence, *inward witness.* Like, how do you know you're saved? There is an inward, deep-down conviction that you can't be convinced otherwise. You know that you know, see? Same principle applies to healing.

The still, small voice is the whisperings of the Spirit to your spirit. As an example, say we're praying for someone who has ulcers. I "hear" in my spirit, *I am administering healing to him.* So I just say, "The Lord is administering healing to you." *I am touching his stomach now.* "He is touching your stomach now." It's slightly different than just an inward prompting. Both are extremely important in accelerating healing. Again, they are developed when we take the time to focus on God within us, honoring Him, worshiping Him, focusing on Him.

The Holy Spirit is the One who helps us facilitate and administrate the release of the Kingdom of God within us. He is the key to seeing the power flow through us, so of necessity that means we need to develop a sensitivity to hearing His voice and being perceptive to His inward leadings. These are simple concepts, but I've met many, many well-meaning Christians who have neglected to develop this inward witness or perceive the still, small voice, and then they wonder why it is so difficult for them to get healed. Not a critical statement at all, just pointing out a need that we *all* should recognize.

Even Jesus, while physically on this earth, was reliant upon the Spirit to help facilitate the release of the Kingdom of God. If it was vitally important that Jesus Himself keep an intimate, close relationship with the Spirit of God, how much more should we as His disciples do the same?

These two attributes of God within us are tremendous keys to releasing His Kingdom for healing and every other aspect of Kingdom promises. What is perceived inwardly in our spirits by the Holy Spirit is, in turn, supposed to be released outwardly to the world at large. We cannot release outwardly what has not been developed inwardly by our close relationship with the Spirit.

As I began to understand these principles—Christ in me, the hope of glory; honoring the inward witness; and developing a sensitivity to the still, small voice—I started feeling more and more of a release of God's power flow out into the person needing ministry. There would be like a surge—*whoom!*—that would let me know the person had been touched. And most of the time, they would feel something too; but you know, if you, as the minister, don't acknowledge that *whoom!*, often the person will wonder if it was simply a warm, ooey-gooey feeling, rather than a divine touch from the Lord. By both of us acknowledging the Lord was moving, it quickened the anointing to accomplish the needed healing or miracle. *Acknowledging the Holy Spirit quickens the healing.*

This confirming that the Spirit is moving is a key to releasing all the gifts—not just healing but the gift of faith, prophecy, word of knowledge, and so on. Many of the Spirit's individual manifestations are perceived through the inward witness and the still, small voice prior to being perceived in the natural realm. By focusing on the Spirit more than the person needing ministry or the need itself, we can begin to cultivate a sensitivity to the Spirit Himself—and by following that focus on the Spirit, at the end we receive whatever manifestation is needed at that time to bring about the release.

Of course we care about the person and the need, but by presenting them (and ourselves) to the Spirit, we give Him "free rein," so to speak, to operate as He sees fit—and of course, He knows exactly the best way to minister to that person in order to set them free.

CHAPTER 14

IT'S RELATIONAL

Early in my ministry, I entered into this type of healing operation in a more formulaic way, and I don't think that's really wrong, we all have to start somewhere. But as time goes on and we develop a deeper sensitivity to the Spirit's prompting, I believe we will find that there is a greater personalization with the Spirit moving through you and me according to our personalities and particular strengths. God is by no means a cookie-cutter kind of God, but these beginning principles are a wonderful place to start developing our own flavor of ministry as we continue to subject ourselves to the Spirit's leading. He is the Guide; we are simply following His promptings.

I am thankful that the Lord doesn't operate in the same, identical way through each person. I said before that in the Bible, Jesus rarely ministered the exact same way to everyone. There is much variety in the movement of the Spirit. There are many diversities of gifts, but it's all the same Spirit (see 1 Cor. 12:4). This is why a word of knowledge, a prophetic word, a gift of faith, or workings of miracles—they all can produce a supernatural manifestation of healing and deliverance. It's really just the Spirit moving upon the person in a unique way and setting them free.

All body ministry is supposed to be an outgrowth of our relationship with Christ; if He didn't operate relationally through us, it would just be formulaic rote. Lay your hands on top their head, recite a few words, and *voila!* healing would come. It would become depersonalized, and the Lord is very much a personal God. So our ability to minister to others is directly related to our personal relationship with Jesus.

I'm glad it's this way, that ministry is birthed out of our relational connection to Christ. Otherwise, we'd simply focus on the formulas for seeing the Spirit move, and we'd lose that vital relationship with Jesus—I in Him and He in me. The whole point of the Christian experience is "that I may know Him" more and more in an ever-increasing manner (Phil. 3:10). It forces us to rely on Him and not a particular mode of operation—the "way we've always done it" kind of thing. I appreciate that God changes things up when He ministers to people.

One of the primary reasons for not seeing a person healed or set free when we pray with them is because we are not walking in a greater expression of the Spirit in our personal lives. James 5:16 declares that the effectual, fervent prayer of a *righteous person* avails much!

Again, I'm not being critical; it's simply a fact we all need to address and press into—a greater, personal revelation of the Lord's Spirit in our lives, which develops godly living, separation unto holiness (see 2 Tim. 2:20-21), and out of that healing, prophecy, and deliverance for others will simply be a byproduct of the internal experiences we are having with Jesus.

None of us have attained, and it will be a lifelong process of learning to walk in the Spirit; but I hope you have come to a dead-set dedication that nothing will stop you from developing a greater sensitivity to the inward witness and the still, small voice of the Lord.

> *That He would grant you, according to the riches of His glory, to be strengthened with might through His Spirit in the inner man, that Christ may dwell in your hearts through faith; that you, being rooted and grounded in love, may be able to comprehend with all the saints what is the width and length and depth and height—to know the love of Christ which passes knowledge; that you may be filled with all the fullness of God* (Ephesians 3:16-19).

This is a key verse to administering and receiving healing because it speaks about intimacy with Christ being the elemental focus to grow in a manifestation of His power. As you encounter His glory in your personal walk with the Lord, you are strengthened in your spirit by His Spirit, who is responding to our faith and love (see Gal. 5:6).

By having these encounters, we are gaining an understanding *with all the saints*—that includes you and me. God expects this of all of us, not just your pastor and the missionaries your church supports. So that we come to a knowledge that passes knowledge. This means a heavenly *knowing* in your spirit that goes beyond earthly head knowledge—a kind of knowledge that is *experienced*, not just known in your brain.

You can know that the sun provides warmth as a scientific fact, but you can only experience that warmth by going out and standing in the sunlight. I've heard James Maloney phrase it this way: "There is a knowing, and then there is a *knowing*."

When your spirit is strengthened by encountering *the* Spirit, you become emboldened to step out and release those things of the Spirit outwardly that you have experienced inwardly. To me, this is the definition of healing ministry. This is not a confidence of the flesh, but rather confidence in Christ. Because you have experienced Him inwardly yourself, you *know* that He will express Himself through you toward someone else. I don't think it's wrong to have a little "spiritual swagger"—a confidence *in Christ* (not in ourselves, for that is fleshly) that He will do what His Word says He will do. We have been changed by our personal relationship with God to give us that kind of kingly/priestly expression. Of course, we know it's not *us*—it's us *in Christ*. But that doesn't negate the truth that He *is* in us, which makes us kingly and priestly because of His kingship and priesthood shining through us (see Rev. 1:6; 5:10).

I believe we need to have a greater revelation of who we are in Christ. Sons, daughters, kings, prophets, priests. It's certainly not a cause to be arrogant, because Christ Himself taught that if we desire to be first, we shall be last (see Matt. 20:26-28). Kingdom dynamics are exactly opposite of the way we think on earth, aren't they? To take this concept of "spiritual swagger" and apply it to ourselves, in our own capabilities and our own expressions, is a surefire way to staunch the flow of Christ in us out into the world.

So of course, keep this all in balance—but it is a truth that we all would do well to begin seeing ourselves as *Christ within us*; it creates an attitude of confidence and expectation. If one really understood and truly believed that Christ was in them, they'd never be afraid to lay hands on someone. And to *not* see that person healed would never enter into their thinking because, hey, Christ *is* in them. False humility, some sense of piety, is just as capable of corroding the expression of Jesus through you as arrogance and pride.

CHAPTER 15

HOW FAITH OPERATES

There have been misconceptions about the gift of faith, and I'd like to take a bit here to try and help clear some of them up, to make it easier to understand. Let me start by sharing about heart miracles and pacemakers dissolving.

Listen, if you're reading this and you have a heart condition or need a pacemaker to disappear—I want you to take it fast! This is to encourage your faith to receive your miracle right now.

Someone will come into the prayer line with a pacemaker. To God's glory and honor, we've seen this kind of miracle so many times, and we'll start giving testimony of Jesus dissolving pacemakers in an effort to make a connection with the person standing in the line. As we share, a connection is formed for this person—a download of faith, as it were. "If Jesus did that a dozen times before, He'll do it for me." Speaking forth these previous testimonies creates an avenue for a gift of faith to be deposited.

This is similar to what we were discussing before concerning the crippled man at Lystra. Remember, it says that he heard Paul speaking, and the apostle observed him intently and saw that he had faith to be healed. Then Paul said "with a loud voice" (Acts 14:10).

There was a connection that Paul "pounced on," so to speak. As faith rises in people, we need to then jump into the mix boldly, declaring the gifts of the Spirit to be released. Again, this is a "take it fast" kind of thing. As Paul spoke the truth forth, faith was created.

That's not to say a river of words creates that gift of faith. Sometimes, we say too much. I know I've talked too much in praying for people in the past. Platitudes: "God loves you, He's touching you, He's here now, He's blessing you," on and on. At some point in time, you're no longer operating in the Spirit but just operating soulishly. Believe me, I know the difference; I did it the wrong way for, like, thirty years. When Dr. Maloney started teaching on "praying too much" or "saying too much," I really took it to heart and started seeing much better results.

Now I may just say, "Lord, thank You for this person." I might not even say it aloud. I try to be led by that inner witness, just thanking God for His grace and then when that impartation hits—"I believe you just got touched, feel where that pacemaker is..."

So the person feels their heart, and we've heard it time and again: "It feels weird. It feels different, soft somehow."

"That's right!" we might say with a "loud voice." "God is touching you right now."

That's the time to step in, that moment of *boom* when faith is rising; this is the time to speak as led by the Spirit, and it is important to speak forth the miracle that the Lord is doing. Don't let those words the person is saying go to waste, because they're stepping into that gift of faith, and you need to boost that faith, being led by the Spirit (not of the soul). Speak it forth: "Keep feeling it. God is moving." And sure enough, the miracle takes place, the pacemaker is dissolved, and praise God—the place comes unglued. Hallelujah!

More often than not, this is the progression of the miracle in faith. The healing virtue *is* there, just on the basis of Christ's atonement; we step into that virtue, proclaiming in faith what God *has* done; the substance of faith is activated by our words, and God responds with the miracle. He is *waiting* to respond with the miracle. He *wants* that person healed.

Keep in mind the focus needs to be on Jesus, not our method, but this is generally how the Lord seems to operate, at least as I've seen it.

The problem I had for thirty years was trying to minister from a soulish standpoint—*I* wanted to see that person healed. And that's a proper motivation, don't get me wrong—we should all *want* to see God move. However, we must realize we can never want to see God move as much as He Himself *wants* to move!

Except, when we pray out of our soulish desire—nothing happens. God's not moved by that, only by our spirit making connection with His. He's waiting on *us* to get out of the soulish realm, get focused on His Spirit, and just watch how quickly He'll move. Take Him fast!

God primarily responds to our faith, even over and above our need. If God responded solely to *need*, this world would look a lot different. But without faith it is impossible to please God (see Heb. 11:6), and that's why Jesus asked, when He comes, would He find faith on the earth (see Luke 18:8). This is in the context of the parable of the persistent widow, and it shows that God responds to faith, not just need.

One of the most powerful ways I've seen faith operate is through praise and worship. We highlighted this briefly a bit earlier, but let's focus more on this.

Giving God glory, honor, praise, and thanks is mentioned often in books on how to receive healing, and yet it remains an often overlooked component, but perhaps it's one of the most important. Because when we praise, it ushers in more of His presence. This is fact: "But You are holy, enthroned in the praises of Israel" (Ps. 22:3). Worship causes His glory to become thicker; His presence is more tangibly felt. This is the *kabod*—"the weightiness of His glory."

I always like ministering in the weightiness of His glory, when faith rises in the room and people are getting healed and it's a celebratory atmosphere. That is when we see the most amazing creative miracles happen, and it's actually easier to see multiple healings taking place simultaneously across the room. Nothing is impossible at that point. That's when we go from having maybe traces of doubt in our hearts to being like, "Yeah! My God can do anything. He's amazing! There's is nothing my God cannot do!" We start to believe what we're singing in those praise songs!

That kind of worship is invigorating. We need to cultivate a habit of staying in that kind of praise attitude. Let the healing flow. Psalms 22:3 declares that God inhabits the praises of His people. As the level of praise increases, so does the glory. Keep giving Him glory and honor. I don't know how to do it any other way, honestly. Because as soon as the praise stops and the anointing dips, I start heading for the exit.

God can work with just a little bit, anything you can give Him. That's all He's asking for, but if there isn't even praise and worship, then you know…

CHAPTER 16

STEPPING INTO FAITH

Jesus went many places during His earthly ministry, and many of the people received Him; but in Nazareth, His hometown, He was virtually shunned. In fact, it was worse than being shunned—they were ready to throw Him off a cliff! We know the story in Luke 4, and it looks like disaster.

But I love the ministry of Jesus! I love the way He opens it up. I study the ministry of Jesus more than anything because Jesus is perfect theology. I learned my theology through Jesus, and I read the epistles through the grid of Jesus.

Like I said before, if we interpret the epistles in the wrong way, contradicting the ministry of Jesus, we get into a real mess, and that's not good. Essentially, we've *robbed* Jesus because we're supposed to be like Him, you know?

Jesus declared, and it was prophesied by Isaiah ahead of time, "But He was wounded for our transgressions, He was bruised for our iniquities; the chastisement for our peace was upon Him, and by His stripes we are healed" (Isa. 53:5).

Can we just settle something? I don't want there to be any doubt in your heart that healing is in the atonement. What Jesus went through with the stripes on His back, it *paid* for your healing. Let's not harp on whether it's His will for you to be healed—I weary of trying to convince saints of something so clearly outlined in the Word of God. Please, let's get beyond that and settle it in our hearts once and for all. Can we agree on that so I don't have to spend fifty pages arguing about how Jesus paid for your healing?

Jesus said of Himself, "The Spirit of the Lord is upon Me, because He has anointed Me to preach the gospel to the poor; He has sent Me to heal the brokenhearted, to proclaim liberty to the captives and recovery of sight to the blind, to set at liberty those who are oppressed; to proclaim the acceptable year of the Lord" (Luke 4:18-19; see also Isa. 61:1-2).

Isn't this an amazing declaration? "To proclaim the acceptable year of the Lord." This is the ministry of Jesus; this is who He is and what He does. He *heals*. Any town that would welcome Him in that capacity saw amazing breakouts of healing.

But He read this passage and was rejected at Nazareth. It was a bad day of ministry—let's call it what it is—but instead of wallowing, what does He do? He goes right on over to the next town, Capernaum.

Here they welcome Him, and Jesus heals Peter's mother-in-law. As a result, the whole town brings all their sick out; *everyone* is healed. I believe your local church, your ministry in whatever capacity you serve, is called to be like Capernaum—a place of healing where people will come and be healed, where you have a reputation of healing and the power of God going forth.

Acts 10:38 talks about, "How God anointed Jesus of Nazareth with the Holy Spirit and with power, who went about doing good and healing all who were oppressed by the devil, for God was with Him."

This is what Jesus did everywhere He went. He knew the quickest way to people's hearts was to heal their bodies. When the people were healed, they realized they were in the presence of greatness, and so many people came to the Lord as a result of that in these towns. Any town that honored Him brought out their sick—they lowered them through roofs, they did whatever they needed to do to get to Jesus.

I want you to note that *they* had to get to Jesus. They didn't just get healed because He came into their town; they had to get to Him.

Bartimaeus cried out, "Jesus, Son of David, have mercy on me!" (Mark 10:47). Remember when we mentioned him earlier? Everyone was like, "Be quiet!" He had to fight through that. He probably embarrassed himself, forcing himself to be heard. I am sure he was thinking, "I don't care what these people think about me. I'm going to declare it—Jesus! Jesus! Jesus! Over here!" And he got Jesus' attention.

Once he got Jesus' attention, the Lord came over and said, "What can I do for you?" and He healed him! Even though people were saying, "Shut up!" it didn't matter to Bartimaeus—he pressed through and got his miracle.

Zacchaeus climbed a tree and got Jesus' attention. Look, I'm not saying it's always easy. I mean, some people had to cut a hole in the roof and lower their friend down to get to Jesus. But whatever it takes to get healed, that's what we need to do. We need to step into faith. No reservation, no hesitancy, not a second thought for the people and circumstances trying to hinder us. Don't let anything stand in your way of stepping into faith!

Jesus is present right now as Jehovah Rapha, Christ the Healer. I've been blessed to have seen so much of His goodness; I've been undone by His love. I've seen too much to ever desire anything other than to see the manifestation of God in healing, to watch His healing power to go forth and revolutionize people's lives. The testimony of Jesus is so powerful!

For the pastors reading this, I want you to be excited about having a healing culture alive and active in your church. This is done by stewarding the testimony of Jesus, training your flock to step into faith no matter what it takes.

I'm reminded of Dennis the pool man; he worked on pools for over twenty years, and his shoulder was shredded to pieces from all the work he'd done. His livelihood was at stake from it.

During one of the healing meetings at our local church, we saw his shoulder get miraculously healed, completely made whole. It totally changed Dennis' life; he was able to go to work without pain. And now he tells everybody about how God healed his shoulder. When he's out taking care of his clients' pools, he has opportunities to pray for them, and people are getting healed all because Dennis' shoulder got healed.

This is the multiplication of the Kingdom. We're stewarding the testimony, and when we have Dennis come up and share how he stepped into faith, it makes his testimony alive and active for anyone who would believe what Jesus did for him to step into that same healing for their own life.

CHAPTER 17

SEIZING THE MOMENT

God gets so much mileage out of these healings; they multiply exponentially. I don't know how He does it and I don't need to, He's God. From one shoulder getting healed, dozens and dozens of shoulders have been healed. From my wife's healing, there have been hundreds and hundreds of people healed based on her testimony of Jesus.

Dear reader, I want to share a little bit more about stepping in. The next time you hear a word of knowledge go forth, let that connect you to the Lord, even if it's not specifically directed toward you. We need to get to a point where we take God fast: "I'm taking this now. I know that God is who He is, and if He's healing others, I'm going to get healed." This needs to be our attitude every time we see God move. There should be an expectancy in our hearts.

See, even though the word of knowledge wasn't specifically yours, you can step into your healing because God's presence is manifest as the word goes out. If He heals one person, He'll heal another—anyone who is willing to step out and take Him fast.

What you don't want to say is, "Oh. The word was for stomach ulcers, and I have a tumor. God must not be here to heal me." See how the enemy tries to talk us out of stepping in and taking our healing? I hate that. I don't want to see that happen, so that's why I mention things like this—to kill all those hindrances. It's really a form of silliness, trying to limit God. *Well, if He's talking about ulcers, He's not talking about tumors.* When in reality, God *is* there, and His presence has manifested to heal. Take Him fast! Seize the moment.

Now, in this present moment is a time to step into faith. Proverbs 13:12 explains, "Hope deferred makes the heart sick, but when the desire comes, it is a tree of life." Hope is good, but when the moment is here, when you feel the presence of God near you, that's time to step into faith and not hope anymore because *hope deferred makes the heart sick.*

Faith is in the *now* moment—it is there to enable you to step into the now. Don't miss this moment. Step into it and avoid any preconceived ideas.

There is so much to learn about this very thing in 2 Kings 5. Naaman was a Syrian, a mighty man of valor who was also a leper. He received word from a servant girl that Elisha operated in healing and miracles. So Naaman said, "*I* want to be healed," and he loaded up his horsemen and chariot and went to go stand in front of the door to Elisha's house.

He got a little "uptight" because Elisha sent out a messenger to meet him—the prophet didn't go himself. And Naaman was a pretty distinguished dude; after all, he came with an entourage.

So he felt a little dissed. Now Elisha's messenger gave him pretty simple instructions—nothing too major here.

> *And Elisha sent a messenger to him, saying, "Go and wash in the Jordan seven times, and your flesh shall be restored to you, and you shall be clean." But Naaman became furious, and went away and said, "Indeed, I said to myself, 'He will surely come out to me, and stand and call on the name of the Lord his God, and wave his hand over the place, and heal the leprosy.'" ...So he turned and went away in a rage* (2 Kings 5:10-12).

Naaman had his own idea about how God was going to heal him. He thought he was calling the shots. "This is what's going to happen: I'm going to show up, he's going to come meet me and wave his magic hand, and I'll be cleansed of leprosy."

But all the servant said was, "Hey, take a dip seven times." That's not too much to ask, is it? Naaman made his healing too complicated when it was really pretty simple—dip seven times, be healed. There was no need to make his healing so complicated. Luckily, his servants were able to talk some sense into the man. He took those dips in the water and was completely restored. How easy was that?

I'm not judging Naaman. I've made healing complicated over the years, too. It's not necessary, and honestly, it can hinder things. Just step in. Just do what the Lord says. Do something you couldn't do before and watch what the Lord does. Watch how He touches. Watch how He cleanses. It's amazing, and it's not overly difficult. Just be willing to follow the simple instructions from the Lord. He's not asking any more of you than He did of Naaman.

I don't know how God's going to work your miracle; I just know He's really good at what He does, and I'm blessed to play whatever role the Lord assigns to me. I'm just trying to establish a connection between you and Him, because I know that if you connect with Him you're going to be healed. Just don't hesitate.

When Jesus healed the ten lepers, all He said was, "Go present yourselves to the priest" and as they went, they were made whole (Luke 17:14). We could say they were healed in that moment when Jesus gave His instruction, but their manifestation didn't occur until they were on their way. That happens in healing a lot. They stepped into it.

You know, we'll do this "five-step prayer model" a lot in meetings. I'll have somebody come up who needs healing to demonstrate this model because the demo person always gets healed.

This one man came up, saying, "I can barely hear out of this ear."

"All right. This is going to be fun. Let's pray for him." And we did, so then I asked him, "How are you doing? Test it out."

"Mmmm. The same."

"Okay. Let's pray again." And I was thinking, *It's going to open the second time.* So I asked, "What happened now?"

"Nothing. It's the same."

"Okay." And we prayed a third time. Still nothing. So I said to the congregation, "Let's just watch what God does. It's not always going to be instantaneous. I've seen this so many times. The key is you pray, you believe, and you watch what God does."

Obviously the congregation was disappointed the healing did not manifest instantly, and they may have even thought it was a failure, but I simply replied, "Just wait and see what God does. We don't know that it was a failure!"

I've learned not to be embarrassed for my God. We just pray. We're just called to go for it and pray for the sick. I don't ask too many questions. I've seen God do too many great things in too many strange ways to think that someone is not going to get healed just because something didn't happen instantly.

You can't necessarily call the way it's going to happen. Naaman tried to call his own shots, and God said something different to him. The Lord has a different way sometimes. That's okay, isn't it? Doesn't God have the right to do that? Can't we just learn to say, "Thank You, God. You have Your own way."

Sure enough, a day or two later the guy testified his ear had completely opened up. Praise God! I said, "Now you can't pretend not to hear your wife anymore when she's talking to you."

CHAPTER 18

I ALSO IMITATE CHRIST

"Imitate me, just as I also imitate Christ." Paul said that in 1 Corinthians 11:1, and there's a real truth in simply duplicating others you've seen who have been used in a healing flow by Jesus. All we are attempting to do is reproduce what the Bible says Christ did. I'm all for greater glory and fresh revelation, but I also would like to see the Body of Christ simply operating how He operated while here on the earth. In many Christian circles, there isn't so much of that happening right now, but praise the Lord, that's changing! This is accelerated healing.

I love how God brings us from glory to glory and takes us higher and higher, but I believe the greater expressions of that development come from when we just focus on ministering how Jesus ministered.

I think stewarding testimonies of healings helps facilitate this endeavor. I love to hear the testimonies that come pouring in—it keeps my faith active and expectant. At our local church, it was the testimonies that got things flowing, and it was stewarding the testimonies that allowed us to become a place known for healing. We've had several words that we're to be a cancer-free zone, and I know that's God's will. Praise God, we're starting to see people come from all over different areas to be healed of various diseases—many people have, indeed, been healed, and we've heard so many great testimonies.

I think the best way to steward healing in your church and to become a place known as having a healing culture in your church is to train up a prayer team that is well-prepared to administer healing—men and women who know their authority and who have prepared themselves to be used by the Lord in a healing operation. This training doesn't happen overnight, but it is vitally important, in my opinion, to accelerate healing; and the first way to start this "healing culture" is to sit under the ministries of others who have been operating in a healing flow. Second, have an ardent desire to steward the testimonies of healing as they start coming in—and they will!

Part of our job as healing ministers is to equip the saints to do the work of the ministry and to help pastors create a culture of healing in their own churches. I hope in the near future we can basically work our way out of a job for each particular church so they don't need "healing ministers" anymore. You know, if we've got to keep coming back to the same place year after year after year in order to see God move in healing, then something's not right. The biblical truth a healing minister is imparting is something that the congregation is supposed to grab hold of. It is to be continually reproduced in the local body, whether or not a traveling healing minister is there.

Accelerated healing is to become a part of who you are, your church's corporate culture, what you all stand for. Healing is a part of who you are because it's a part of who Jesus is and He's in you. He is the Head; you are His Body—and the head and the body need to be acting in unison, otherwise something is out of order. All churches need to be healing churches—that's simply a fact of charismatic Christian theology.

To be biblically correct here, let's state it as "Christ is in you by the Holy Spirit." That is a fact of being born again, further ignited by being baptized in the Holy Spirit with the evidence of speaking in tongues.

I'm absolutely thrilled by the testimonies of healing that are consistently coming in. That shows me there is a continuing shift of the "wineskin" of modern Christendom. Praise the Lord for this! So by sharing testimonies throughout this book, my journey into healing as it were, I trust in the Spirit that He will create within you the desire to relate to this type of expression and begin to duplicate it within your own spheres of influence. My desire is to help you grow into an acceleration of healing. Even reading these types of materials can give you a huge impartation of God's grace manifesting through you as you mix what you're reading with faith. I am convinced you're going to notice a big difference when you go out and pray for the sick from this time forward.

God will set you up sometimes. These are divine appointments that God creates, opportunities for Him to flow through you as you go about your day-to-day life. Sometimes these setups are very clear and you're aware that, "Wow! This is a divine appointment, and God's doing this."

Other times, it seems like *you* are creating the opportunities by sticking yourself out there (like walking up to a guy in a wheelchair at the grocery store), but then you realize it was actually a God thing the whole time. They're *all* divine setups. It's just that you've trained yourself not to miss it, to be more aware of the Spirit's subtle promptings. He rarely will crack you over the head with a spiritual hickory stick and shout in your ear, "Pray for *that* person!"

God doesn't have to blare His intentions really, really loudly in order to make Himself crystal clear—though I admit sometimes He's had to do that with me on occasion. But I'm learning and growing in this! And I hope you are too!

That's why iron sharpens iron (see Prov. 27:17). I learn something every time I'm with an anointed minister of God such as James Maloney and Randy Clark; I started out a lot by imitation. I just did it how they did it, and the Lord honored me as He honored them, all of us for honoring His Word and His Spirit.

I used to teach (and still do) the so-called "Five Step Prayer Model" a lot in services; I think it was developed under the Vineyard model. I don't know if you've seen that done in your church, but it's basically five steps to pray for the sick. It provided some great guidelines on how to start out praying for healing, and I didn't ever veer from that when starting out. But then, the more people I prayed for, the more I was stepping into ministry, the more I started to hear God's voice directing me what to do.

It's by reason of use that you begin to develop sensitivity more and more to how the Lord talks to you specifically (see Heb. 5:14). Everybody hears and sees a little bit differently because we're all unique individuals in the Lord. Of course, God never contradicts His own Word, but just as you are capable of great variety, so is He. As you grow and develop, you begin to recognize patterns in the way He moves in your particular life.

I know many ministers who started out just as I did, by imitating the ones who had gone before them. I imitated Dr. James and the way he ministered. He would do it, I would do it the same way, and I would get very similar results because I was with him.

He started out by imitating what he saw from those great healing ministries of the Jesus Movement. There was an anointing with those ministries that came upon him, and as I ministered with him I began to perceive I was coming under the anointing on his life.

Then, after a season of growing and developing, the anointing began to show itself in a customized way through my ministry. Ministry grows into a customized expression of who you are as a unique individual in the Lord's Body. That's an acceleration of the healing anointing, see? But the vast majority of us didn't start out that way. We started out by imitation.

In fact, it's probably not good to start out trying to be "unique." Sometimes there's too much emphasis on a personal expression when, in reality, *all* of us are simply imitating Christ.

I understand why people say, "You'll only be a good you; you'll never be a good anybody else," and I agree with it—we are supposed to be individuals, not carbon copies. But a certain level of character development and breaking upon the Rock of Christ, as well as a time of instruction and "serving in another's vineyard," is required before He will entrust to us our own personal level of expression. Starting out, it's okay to be a copycat.

That's why Paul said, "Imitate me as I imitate Christ." It's as if he was saying, "Just do what I do for a while, and you'll be in good shape." That's why these men and women of God have come before us—to provide examples, as they are an example of the One great Example, the Lord Jesus Christ. How can we stand on the shoulders of giants if we're trying to be unique and not minister like anybody else? It's a contradiction in some ways, isn't it?

CHAPTER 19

A CONSTANT SHIFT

As I imitated, God began to open doors and things began to shift, and they are always shifting. I'm still growing each and every time I minister to someone. I've held many, many healing meetings, and every time I do God teaches me something new. I'll go back to the hotel, and it's almost like a debriefing sometimes. God says, "Remember that? When I did that?"

"Yeah. What was that?"

"Well, this is what I wanted you to do, okay?"

"Oh. Okay, God. I'll try to get that one next time."

Accelerated healing is learning to be led by the Spirit as you grow and develop. Impartations will really aid your life and ministry, but to maximize one's effort requires living a life led by the Spirit. And that means it will be a constant state of shifting, growing, stretching in the Lord. Sometimes that can be uncomfortable; it's human nature to want to "coast"—do things the easy way we've always done them before. And there's a truth to this concept. Don't fix what isn't broken.

But I'm saying that as you put what you've learned to use, watch how God starts changing things up on you. Watch what God does. He's multifaceted, and we can never stagnate in the name of staying within our comfort zone. Be willing to change as the Spirit directs you. Be always learning, always pressing, always increasing.

I remember in one service a woman gave testimony of the Lord touching her during the previous service. God had been ministering to knees. We'll call this woman Nina for privacy's sake. Even when Nina was a little girl, she'd always had knee problems. Oddly, her knees would ache during her sleep, and the pain would wake her up; she'd lose sleep from it. Flash forward some twenty years, and it was still the same thing. That's a *long* time to be losing sleep because your knees are throbbing!

In fact, the night before God touched her, she couldn't sleep because of the pain in her knees. After the Lord moved, she slept like a baby and gave testimony the next night, "God had to wake me up!"

Come on, Jesus!

She went on to say that the enemy had been attacking her mind the past year, and the night she left the conference she was in tears, battling for a breakthrough. She kept pressing in, praising and worshiping the Lord all the next day, and suddenly she testified that she felt "drenched" in the oil of the Holy Spirit. Something broke and the Spirit delivered her mind from all the stuff the enemy had been attacking her with for over a year.

See, that's accelerated healing! Not only did God touch her physical needs, He set her free emotionally and mentally as well.

That's why when I pray for people I sometimes say, "Lord, make them totally whole." I believe that's how Jesus operated, and I want to see the same things accomplished by Him through my ministry.

There's a developing shift in the Body as a whole toward this "complete work" when we minister to others. I think the Lord really wants us to focus on seeing people completely set free. We focus a lot on physical healing, and that's, of course, perfectly correct. But what happened to Nina when that oil covered her and broke off the mental harassment as well as healed what had been wrong with her knees for decades.

Maybe you are dealing with something similar. We've seen so many people get a breakthrough in these areas—sometimes there can be a physical issue accompanying it, but a lot of times it's a constant mental harassment, a consistent "block" in a certain area of life. It's like they'll hit an emotional/mental wall. "Man. There's that thing again!" These things are not always easily identifiable, nor are they the root cause. "Every time I think this is finally going, it rears its ugly head." Depression. Fatigue. Frustration. We all face emotions and expressions like this from time to time based on our circumstances, but for many people out there they simply can't put their finger on "what's wrong." So medical science prescribes medications, and this does indeed help some people, but it often treats the symptoms, not the cause.

I am sure at least some of you reading this can relate to what I'm describing. Ultimately, whether the root is emotional, physical, or mental, these are areas in one's life that need to be broken through. The Spirit of God wants His people set free in every area of their lives. Accelerated healing is the type of ministry that Jesus portrayed while on this earth. Above and beyond, a rapid progression toward total health and wellbeing. Not only were physical limitations, diseases, and sicknesses dealt with but also every other kind of issue that people faced—mental harassments, the constant nagging in the back of the mind, the ever-present patterns that kept coming up in one's life.

They are often called strongholds; sometimes they can be iniquities passed down from generation to generation (physical conditions like diabetes, mental disorders, or alcoholism).

It's often a physical thing, but it could be a repeated issue someone is facing, financial desperation, struggles in the mind, overwhelming emotional unbalances. Whatever it happens to be—anything you can identify that is plaguing you—let the Holy Spirit put His hand on that thing right now. We want to deal with that thing once and for all and be done with it.

It is my expectation as you're reading this material and mixing it with faith that the Spirit will set you free. That's what it's all about! God made His sons and daughters to be free to step into the abundant life He provided. This is the law of life of the Spirit in Christ Jesus that Romans 8 speaks about. This shift in the Spirit is moving the entire Body of Christ into this type of abundant life.

I remember there was a really cool moment that happened to me at a little convenience store/gas station. It's just normal life sometimes, you know—you're going about your day when these "divine setups" occur. I was going in to pay the cashier. (Yes, I'm one of those guys who still pays cash for everything.) Suddenly, the presence of God showed up in the place in a very tangible way. I thought to myself, "Oh! That's God's presence!"

It's one thing when the presence of God falls upon you while you're praying in private. That's important to have those moments. But when God "shows up" in a public place, you have to realize it's not just for you. He's creating a "special moment" for the people around you. There's a *reason* why you feel Him fall in the grocery store or the restaurant. The more I grew to realize this, the more I recognized these are divine "setup" moments.

So I looked at the cashier. He looked at me. I can't say that he felt the presence of God, but obviously he must have sensed something because we both looked at each other like, "Whoa. What's going on here?"

I didn't ask permission to pray for him. I just broke all the protocols, right? Sometimes it's okay to do this when you're honoring the person God is leading you to. It takes boldness, and I'm not saying go clunk someone over the head because you "felt" the Spirit moving. There is wisdom and discernment here, but sometimes when you're drunk in the Holy Ghost and His presence is there, you do funny things. This was being orchestrated by Him. So I just blurted out, "God's doing something," without thinking anything through. It just came out of my mouth. "He's touching your breathing. You've got a breathing issue."

The cashier gasped in shock. "Yeah."

"So take a deep breath."

He started taking deep breaths. "Oh, my..."

I nodded. "The Lord just healed you."

"I can breathe! This is amazing."

"Thank You, God." And then I paid the man.

This is a great time to preach and share the gospel with people as their hearts are opened by the miracle encounter with God and their ears are ready to receive truth.

This is the shift I believe we are all heading into. Accelerated healing. And I believe more divine setups like this are going to increase in your life!

CHAPTER 20

MOVED WITH COMPASSION

What I want to share with you is really about the heart. The more intimate we are with the Lord, the more we understand His flow and the way He moves. I love what Matthew 14:14 says, "When Jesus went out He saw a great multitude; and He was moved with compassion for them, and healed their sick."

I want us to see how those two things go together. First He was "moved with compassion." What was the result of being moved with compassion? He healed their sick.

Did you know healing the sick is something every believer can do? According to Mark 16:17, Jesus said, "These signs will follow those who believe." Notice He didn't say, "These signs will follow those with gifts of healing."

Jesus said of all believers, "They will lay hands on the sick, and they will recover." No one is excluded from that statement. That's all of us who believe. Every one of you. Look at your hands and say, "These are healing hands."

"These signs will *follow*" means everywhere you go, you leave a wake of healing behind you—people being healed, set free, and delivered in your path. That's accelerated healing!

So what's one of the keys? God's looking for your compassion. And what is compassion, you ask? Simply put, compassion is focused agape love. Think of compassion like a magnifying glass for love.

There are a couple words in the original Hebrew and Greek that I want to share with you that really describe what's happening when you pray for the sick.

We can think of the first word as the *potential energy* of God—that is, the love of God that is the catalyst that starts the chain reaction. The things that God is working in you by the power of His Spirit are all catalyzed by His unwavering love for you. His miraculous power manifesting to the external world is the expression of that love flowing outward to others. The Hebrew word pertaining to this potential energy is *gibbor*, which we could translate as "mighty power." The Greek translation would be *kratos*. We all carry *gibbor/kratos* by the power of the Holy Spirit residing within us.

The release of that potential is a different Greek word, *dynamis*, which we can think of as *kinetic energy*.

So there's *kratos*, what's already resident within each Spirit-filled believer, and *dynamis*, the release of it. The point here is, it's one thing to *have* power (potential energy), and it's another thing to release it (kinetic energy). They are two different things, but they both refer to the same power of God. It's the same power, but one expression is inside you; the other is an expression released to others. So when the person gets healed, saved, set free, delivered, whatever—that's the release of *kratos* in a *dynamis* expression.

So an element of accelerated healing comes when we recognize the resident power of God inside us and express it to those in need.

The question, then, is how do we get to that point where what we have within us, the *kratos* power of the Spirit of God, is released outward in a *dynamis* explosion to affect others around us? And the answer is focused love, compassion—that is, following the flow of love that God has extended to every human being on the planet, whether they return it to Him or not.

In that moment in the gas station (from the last chapter), I felt a flow of love that was only God toward the cashier. I didn't know that guy from Adam; he was a twenty-something young man I'd never met before. But you learn over time, the more you do it, the more you walk in it, the more you surrender to it, you see the flow of love that the Lord directs. It's when you love that you begin to see the accelerated healings.

Throughout these years of ministry, praying for the sick, I realize more and more that it is the person standing in front of me that matters. In that moment of initiating an encounter with God, that person is the most important person in the world. There is nobody more important than the person standing in front of me at that moment, because that's the person who's *here*. That's the person I'm to pray for—the one standing before me who needs to receive from God. That makes them very special in that moment. The Creator of all existence has turned His sole attention on that one precious man or woman.

But if my mind is here, there, everywhere instead of solely focused on the one before me, it's like saying, "Okay. Well, be blessed. Thanks for coming out." I have the power of the Holy Spirit in me, but is it being released into that person? Not necessarily.

As soon as I focus my love on the Lord and I get the Lord's perspective of that person—what he or she means to Him—that's when the prophetic words come, that's when the release of the glory flows into that person, and the healing is accelerated. It's love being projected on someone's needs. We care because God cares.

That's why I say, "Thank You, God, that You have given me Your love, Your heart," before I minister because I know that if I acknowledge what God says I have by His Spirit, the people will be touched. I don't want to be distracted and minister out of the wrong place; it only produces spotty results—half-breakthroughs at best. But the release of the power of God projected through divine love, that'll break through any barrier, overthrow any stronghold, bind any strongman. That's why Jesus, as the God/Man, was so good at what He did, because He was so full of love. Jesus is perfect love, and He knows how to release the love of His Father into the people as He prays for them.

I'll never forget an admonitory story that James Maloney shared with me. He was in a prayer meeting once. (He's done thousands and thousands of these healing services, no exaggeration, so he knows what he's talking about.) All of a sudden, he felt a surge of God's power come upon him. He thought, *Whoa! I'm getting it. There's the anointing! I feel God's power.* So he thought the Spirit wanted to move, and he started laying hands on people so the anointing would come upon them. Wouldn't you do the same thing?

People in the congregation were falling out, getting blasted, drunk in the Holy Ghost, having just a great time in the Lord, almost being silly from this move of the Spirit. Now, I love meetings like that. I love it when things *happen*, and there's time set aside for that—they're wonderful times of refreshing, don't misunderstand me. We always have to follow the flow of love and be in tune with the Holy Spirit, what He wants to do in that moment. It's all about living in the moment in God—constant fellowship with Him.

But after everyone had this great time of laughter and joy and refreshing, Dr. James got back behind the pulpit as the people started coming to, and he got a rebuke from the Holy Spirit: "You weren't listening to Me! You didn't ask Me what to do with that expression in that moment! Do you see that crippled person in the front row? I gave you that surge of anointing for that person to get healed. But you weren't listening, and you went around and splashed it all over the place!"

I get chills every time I repeat that story he shared with me. Oh, Lord Jesus, help us to focus Your love as You want it to be focused! We don't ever want to miss a moment with God. He has so much grace and forgiveness for us, and we're all still learning to follow the flow of love. It will always direct us to the right person at the right time! That is accelerated healing.

CHAPTER 21

TOSSING OUT JUNK AND EXPRESSING LOVE

These are the kinds of things we learn in ministry as we grow in the Lord, as we set aside our own *junk*. That's why it's important for you to get healed of your own junk. I'm not being mean here; we all have junk to deal with, so I'm not picking on you. And if you don't think you have junk to deal with, then *that* is your junk to deal with! ⊠

As you learn to toss out these hindrances that keep you from living moment to moment in God, you find you don't have to think about *yourself* as much. You can really focus on Him. And when you focus on Him, He gives you a heart for other people. That's the way our Kingdom is designed. I know I said "our Kingdom," and yes, it's the Kingdom of God; but He's decided to share it with us, so now it's also "our Kingdom." And it's important we take good care of it—don't leave junk piles sitting around, you know?

The New Covenant is such an amazing thing! It completely blows me away. I thank You, God, that it's all about sonship. I'll share more on sonship a little later. For now, let's agree that God is going to set you up with these *moments*, opportunities to convert the potential energy inside you to kinetic energy outside you; and it's when you communicate with Him, when you learn to receive love from Him all during the day, your junk is tossed away, and more of that divine energy can flow out of you.

There's a great activation exercise I've seen done a lot in ministry schools. You take out a piece of paper and ask God what He thinks about you. Basically start a journal. It's a good way to get the flow of how God thinks, how He's speaking to you. "I love you. You're My son, you're My daughter. I have a plan and a purpose for your life."

When you start to hear what God says to you all the time, that's when you begin to hear what God is thinking about *other* people. Once you've developed that for yourself, once you learn to receive His love, you're able to project that love outward to others. You need to receive love first before you express love focused on the needs of others. It becomes so much easier to have His heart for other people, to share His love with them, when we have learned to receive that love for ourselves.

This is such an important key to accelerated healing. It's a key to the prophetic, to receiving words of knowledge. The gifts of the Spirit are not really "for us." If I have a gift of words of knowledge, does that really benefit me? I suppose I could get a word of knowledge for myself, but you know what I mean. Usually we don't need words of knowledge concerning ourselves. So predominately it's for others. The expressions of the gifts of the Spirit are mostly for others; the fruit of the Spirit is for ourselves and others. We all play our parts in the Body of Christ, and this is how the Bride is going to become spotless and beautiful. I need you to toss out your junk and express God's love just as much as you need me to toss out my junk and express God's love. We need each other to "do it right."

I care so much about the Church. I love the Church because Jesus loves the Church. I can't stand it when anyone speaks badly about the Church. I hear people say all the time, "I've been burned by the Church for this and that."

Look, I know the Church is far from perfect because I'm in it, and you're in it, and we all have junk that needs to be processed. But *nobody* was burned by "the Church" worse than Jesus, and He gave His life for it. Ephesians 5:25 says that Jesus loved the church (*ecclesia*) and gave His life for it.

Think about that. Sometimes people feel like they don't even want to *go* to church. "I don't want to go to church because they're this and that." Insert some negative, derogatory thought here. I bet you've said that at least once in your Christian walk; I know I have. But let's call a spade a spade. We're speaking badly about something that Christ *died* for—His Bride. Fellas, what would you think if someone said that about *your* bride? And here's the kicker—if you're born again, *you* are part of that Bride, so you're really talking badly about yourself. See, it's junk! And it inhibits the expression of love, not only to others in the Bride but to those out there who haven't yet joined the Bride.

Jesus is coming back for a pure and spotless Bride. We do our part by following His flow of love. We simply *follow* it. We aren't creating it; we can't! We enter into His love, and then we have love for other people. Then it's not so bad—people don't push our buttons as much, and we're able to impact their lives more for the glory of God. That's how body ministry is supposed to operate, and if we're not seeing it like that then maybe we're not loving like we should. Just a thought.

The Lord was betrayed by those He loved the most—how terrible that must've been. He was abandoned and rejected by His own. None of the disciples, except for John, were around after He got arrested. Peter was *sort of* there, but he denied he even knew the Man. Judas betrayed Him. The Bible doesn't mention much about where the others were; it just says they fled and deserted Him.

But John was there. Interesting to note he's the disciple whom Jesus loved (see John 13:23). John the Beloved. Do you think there's a connection between John being around at the end when nobody else was and him calling himself the disciple whom Jesus loved?

He tapped into something none of the other disciples were able to during the time that Jesus was with them. Eventually, we know all the early apostles learned to receive and express love, but it was John who was leaning against Jesus at the Last Supper—the one originally called a "Son of Thunder" (which most likely means he had an anger issue to start with).

As important as all of the apostles were to the Body of Christ, John has a special place as "the Beloved," to whom was given the Revelation, and the only disciple of the original twelve to not be martyred. I want to be like John, don't you?

The greatest key to the miraculous is learning to receive and express love. When you start to receive love from your Father, nothing is impossible. That's when you get healed. That's when you get set free. That's when you begin to know who you are—that you are who He says you are! That's the bottom line. You're not who the world says you are. You're not who the person who rejects you when you try to tell them about Jesus says you are. You are who He says you are, and that's it.

When you learn to recognize and believe that truth and you begin to align yourself with who you truly are in Christ, then you begin to get set free from yourself, and you're able to follow the flow of love better.

I don't have this all figured out; I'm still learning and will continue to do so till I meet my Lord face to face. But I'm learning! And I want you to learn this too. I say to God, "Lord, thank You for giving me Your heart to see with Your eyes." By acknowledging what God has already done, you position your mind to receive from the mind of Christ (see 1 Cor. 2:16).

Jesus said, "I only do what I see My Father do" (see John 5:19), and everything Jesus did was amazing, and it was focused, projected love. So obviously all He's doing is seeing His Father love on people. He's seeing through His Father's love eyes. That's all ministry is, and it's probably the greatest key to accelerated healing—connecting people to God through your love. You've got the Father's heart and the Father's eyes through the work of the Holy Spirit, and you're simply loving on them. If they're receiving that love, then they will be healed, set free, or delivered. Because of your encounter with God's love turned outward and focused on the needs of people, it's like they are receiving love directly from the Father in those moments of connection. Then they're wrecked by that love and completely transformed.

> *And now abide faith, hope, love, these three; but the greatest of these is love* (1 Corinthians 13:13).

What that dear sister from earlier, Nina, was describing was liquid love. She felt an anointing go down her head and set her free from all that junk that was hindering the flow of love in her heart. We, too, should be stepping into the flow of love!

CHAPTER 22

THE WAY JESUS DID IT

A lot of times, when we pray for people and they testify to feeling an initial release of anointing in their bodies, there is a period of time when their bodies are mending. Many times, we'll receive testimony later saying the healing or miracle was completed.

You might find yourself in a similar situation. Your body may need a little time to mend, and that's okay. Laugh at it, and let the anointing continue its work to amend what's wrong. I mention this so you don't fall into the trap of discouragement if your healing is not instantaneous. While I believe that we are approaching a season in the Lord that really accelerates instantaneous healing, we cannot dictate that *every* healing occurs on the spot.

Sometimes it takes a little bit of time, and there's no reason to be disheartened. If you sensed the power of God touch your body, He's not leaving you hanging; there is a process of mending. Sometimes your body needs to adjust. If you're used to favoring one side of your body—I don't know, let's say you had a leg or hip out of place, and now the Lord's shifting it back but you're used to walking funny—there can be a little bit of time for your body to adjust to being healed.

We are all pressing in for instant healings—that's not a cop out. That's scriptural. When Jesus raised up Jairus' daughter, she was obviously still weak. He said, "Get her something to eat," implying even though she'd been raised from the dead, she hadn't eaten in a long time, so her body was still weak (see Mark 5:43). Otherwise, why tell her folks to get her some food? Actually, it was a sign that a miracle itself had taken place that she was even able to eat in the first place. If you're dead, you aren't hungry.

My point is, don't get discouraged if it takes your body a little while to mend and fully recover.

I want to share a bit more of my journey into healing ministry by starting with a couple verses that talk about how Jesus ministered while on the earth.

> *And Jesus went about all Galilee, teaching in their synagogues, preaching the gospel of the kingdom, and healing all kinds of sickness and all kinds of disease among the people. Then His fame went throughout all Syria; and they brought to Him all sick people who were afflicted with various diseases and torments, and those who were demon-possessed, epileptics, and paralytics; and He healed them. Great multitudes followed Him—from Galilee, and from Decapolis, Jerusalem, Judea, and beyond the Jordan* (Matthew 4:23-25).

This is the ministry of Jesus, and for me *everything* is Jesus. The ministry of Jesus is what I strive for. I just love the way He laid His life down for the people around Him, even though He went through a lot of persecution for it. Understand when you say "the ministry of Jesus" it's not all physical healing, though that is the majority of His earthly ministry. But there are certainly other things that go along with that.

The above verse says that Jesus went throughout all Galilee. Picture this: He was teaching in the synagogues, proclaiming the good news of the Kingdom—He delivered a Kingdom message. And then it says He healed every type of disease and sickness among the people. I want you to see that—Kingdom message, healing the sick.

Then the Bible says news about Him spread all over Syria, and people brought to Him all who were ill with various diseases and torments.

I love the matter-of-fact statement: "He healed them." Those with severe pain came, and their pain left. Those who had demons, the demons were cast out. Folks with seizures, paralytics. All were healed.

Awesome! This concept of accelerated healing goes beyond "getting healed quickly," as important as that is. This book is trying to show a progression into a fuller manifestation of *everything* Jesus did in His earthly ministry.

What was the result of His healing "all kinds" of things that plagued the people? "Great multitudes followed Him—from Galilee, and from Decapolis, Jerusalem, Judea, and beyond the Jordan" (Matt. 4:25). The Bible says the "fame" of Jesus spread—that's accelerated healing! That's the ministry of Jesus.

Let's fast forward to the end of Mark's Gospel now.

> *And He said to them, "Go into all the world and preach the gospel to every creature. He who believes and is baptized will be saved; but he who does not believe will be condemned. And these signs will follow those who*

> *believe: In My name they will cast out demons; they will speak with new tongues; they will take up serpents; and if they drink anything deadly, it will by no means hurt them; they will lay hands on the sick, and they will recover." So then, after the Lord had spoken to them, He was received up into heaven, and sat down at the right hand of God. And they went out and preached everywhere, the Lord working with them and confirming the word through the accompanying signs. Amen* (Mark 16:15-20).

Jesus showed His disciples how the ministry was supposed to work. Accelerated healing in action. He not only spoke *about* the Kingdom, but there was a demonstration of that Kingdom to back up His words. The gospel of Jesus Christ is not just in words, but in power (see 1 Cor. 4:20). That's just the way our Kingdom is, and it's set up wonderfully if I do say so myself!

In the first part of the above passage, Jesus is just highlighting all the things He did Himself. It's the same operation—the exact same way Jesus worked before. The second part of that passage shows that Jesus sat down at the right hand of God—I love that! He's watching over our proceedings, seeing if we'll do the same things He did!

But notice He's not left it all up to us! "They will speak with new tongues," refers to the indwelling of His Holy Spirit. We have been empowered by Him to operate as the Lord did. Ever noticed how the deliverance portion of that comes first? "They will cast out demons," and then, "They will speak with new tongues." That shows me there is often an element of deliverance that needs to occur before the infilling of the Spirit empowers our ministry.

Next the Bible says, "They went out and preached everywhere." Boldness. Deliverance, infilling, boldness, demonstration. In that order. Listen to this: "The Lord working with them and confirming the word through the accompanying signs." This shows a co-laboring. Again, I want to point out, we do the small possible, and He does the large impossible. It's still *Jesus* confirming the word with signs, but He's working through a group of people who have committed themselves to duplicating their Master's works. And the book ends with, "Amen." So be it. I say amen too!

The word has to be confirmed with the accompanying signs. It's not enough to say that He's the Healer. There needs to be a *demonstration* that He is the Healer. Prove it! It's not enough to say that He has conquered evil; you have to cast the demons out of people! It's a great picture—Jesus does it all; He demonstrates the validity of His words.

Remember when Jesus was baptized by John, a voice from heaven said, "This is My beloved Son, in whom I am well-pleased" (Matt. 3:17). My wife, Janet, points out an interesting thought in Matthew 11, when John sent two of his disciples to inquire if Jesus was, indeed, the Coming One (the Messiah, in other words). Notice that Jesus does not say, "Well, John was there when My Father spoke out of heaven. Obviously, I'm the Son God."

Instead, He says, "Go and tell John the things which you hear and see: The blind see and the lame walk; the lepers are cleansed and the deaf hear; the dead are raised up and the poor have the gospel preached to them. And blessed is he who is not offended because of Me" (Matt. 11:4-6).

Jesus proved the validity that He was the Coming One based on the demonstration of His Kingdom—not just His words, but His actions. Too often we are telling the people of the world who *we* are ("I am a Christian," "I am a child of God") and they don't really care—they need healing, not words. We need to be demonstrating who *He* is, not who *we* are.

Jesus didn't really go around a lot saying, "I'm the Messiah; I'm the Son of God." Usually, He referred to Himself as the "Son of Man." We should act in like manner—not referring to ourselves, but Jesus working through us in demonstration of the Kingdom's power.

This is why He informed the disciples, "It's better if I go to the Father and send the Holy Spirit to you." In essence, He said, "Tag. You're it. It's your turn now." He goes to be with the Father, and it's our turn now to fulfill the ministry of Jesus. Isn't that amazing?

CHAPTER 23

NOW IT'S OUR TURN

It's *our* task. Jesus has given it to us. And we're empowered by the *same* Holy Spirit, the *same* way that Jesus was, so that we can operate the *same* way. Why is it better, though, if He goes to the Father? Ever wondered that? Wouldn't it *seem* better to have Him stay here, hang out, and do it for us?

Well, we get the double bonus! Not only do we get the Holy Spirit like Jesus had Him, but we also have Jesus interceding for us in heaven! That's one thing Jesus didn't have. Yes, of course, Jesus had the Holy Spirit and the Father, but now that He has ascended, in His glorified role as King of all creation, *we* have the Spirit with Jesus interceding for us, and therefore we have access to the Father! What a wonderful progression! That's accelerated healing, isn't it?

Okay. So I read those verses in Mark 16. I was like, "That's awesome. I love it, that's incredible. I think I believe it. I sort of believe it, but see, if I believe it..." and I started praying for the sick. I'd go to the hospitals and pray for people who were dying, *hoping* they'd get well.

I'd have friends who were sick. People would ask me, "John, why don't you go lay hands on them? We want you to pray for them," and I'd pray for them, *hoping* they wouldn't die, and they would still die. It was so heartbreaking for me.

Then I would pray for others. I'd pray for people who *weren't* dying, and they would die. It got bad, like assisted suicide if I laid hands on you. If someone *wanted* to die, they'd be like, "Let's call John in." I joke about it now, but it was almost that bad, like I was performing last rites or something. "*In nomine Patris....*" In Jesus' name, you're healed. Boop. Dead. It really was like that for *years.* How sad is that? As I say it now, it's kind of funny, but really it was just heart-wrenching. You can imagine the disappointment. I can't be the only person who's ever been disappointed with healing and praying for the sick.

Then, I'd try to cast out a demon, because the verse in Mark 16 said to go cast out demons. I'd speak to the demon, "Go!"

"No!"

"I said, go in Jesus' name!"

"I don't want to!"

Ugh. That's not good, right? Was it ever hard for Jesus to cast out a demon? No. Was it ever hard for Jesus to heal anybody? No. So what's going on here?

> *Now may the God of peace Himself sanctify you completely; and may your whole spirit, soul, and body be preserved blameless at the coming of our Lord Jesus Christ* (1 Thessalonians 5:23).

I love that. "May the God of peace Himself." So good! But what I want you to see here is how Scripture distinguishes that we are made up of three parts—spirit, soul, and body. You are not just *you* as a body. You have a spirit, you have a soul, and you have a body. We know these bodies; God heals them, but should the Lord tarry, they go eventually. It's a fact. Unless the Lord returns in our lifetimes (and we all pray He does), all of us will at one point face physical death. Death is the last enemy to be defeated, and that only occurs when Jesus returns and sets His feet on the Mount of Olives.

But the great thing is we're promised new, glorified bodies. This body gets replaced, but we keep the soul and we keep the spirit. But you know I'm going to look a *lot* better when I get my glorified body. Probably so will you. Praise God for that!

Spirit, soul, and body. Peter calls the spirit "the hidden man of the heart" (1 Pet. 3:4 KJV). That's what he was referring to—your spirit. Other translations have it "the inner man" or "the inner self." That's your spirit. When you are born again, the Holy Spirit comes in and resides with your spirit. Spirit and spirit. That's all good.

You have everything in the spirit because you have the Holy Spirit, and your spirit feeds on the Holy Spirit. It's all there. It's resident. It is within you. The Kingdom of God is where? That's right, it's in you! That's what Colossians 1:27 means: "Christ in you, the hope of glory." We have Christ in us.

> *For I through the law died to the law that I might live to God. I have been crucified with Christ; it is no longer I who live, but Christ lives in me; and the life which I now live in the flesh I live by faith in the Son of God, who loved me and gave Himself for me. I do not set aside the grace of God; for if righteousness comes through the law, then Christ died in vain* (Galatians 2:19-21).

So how did I begin to overcome being the man formerly known as "God's least anointed"? I mean, based on my past history and track record, I should be the least qualified person to be standing up there ministering healing to someone. That's not the case anymore, so what made all the difference in the world for me?

Part of the answer is I received two significant impartations in my life. (I'll discuss these in a bit.) Prior to these, I was so frustrated over the years with my lack of healing. I knew the problem wasn't God. I knew the problem was me, but I didn't know how to fix *me*. What was happening this whole time I was praying for the sick and not seeing results?

I was believing when I prayed for the sick. "If I just believe...if I just believe they're going to get healed, they're going to get healed."

Well, believing is in your mind, and your mind is part of your soul. Your soul is your mind (including the *way* you think), your will, and your emotions, which are all separate from the spirit man.

I was thinking in my mind, "If I just believe they'll get healed, they'll get healed," and they didn't get healed because it was a mind game. It was praying out of my mind, and that won't get people healed because that's coming out of the soul (again—mind, will and emotions comprise the "soul"). The soul is not "evil" per se, but it is not a spiritual entity; it is very much a part of this natural world just as your body is. God gave you a soul for a reason; He wants you to use your brain and your emotions, provided your will is submitted to His Spirit. Your soul just needs to be renewed by the Spirit living within your spirit through the washing of water by the Word (see Rom. 12:2; Ep. 5:26).

But the soul cannot make anyone healed. It takes the *spirit* to receive spiritual matters, and healing is a spiritual thing.

So what happened all those years I was praying for the sick with my soul is I was taking in stuff from the world and try to filter it through my mind and five senses to *make* healing work. Bottom line, my soul is cluttered with stuff from the world and all this natural stuff around me. Even if this natural stuff isn't all "sinful," it's still just natural, not supernatural.

Living in this world, I'm taking stuff into my body through my senses—seeing, hearing, smelling, listening to things I shouldn't. And again, not everything "natural" is inherently evil; the Bible says the earth and everything in it is the Lord's according to Psalms 24:1. However, all of creation is groaning (see Rom. 8:22). This tells me that the natural world is tainted by a law of sin and death (see Rom. 8:2).

Thankfully, we have been redeemed from this law by the Law of the Spirit of life in Christ Jesus, but even though we may not be "of this world," we certainly are *in* it (see John 15:19; 17:14-16). So maybe the stuff of the world is resident in the soul. This is the lifetime process of being renewed in the thinking of our minds as we submit to the work of the Holy Spirit.

So back then, when I was praying for people out of my soul, it was filtered by all the stuff that had built up in there. I'm not sure how it had all gotten there. I certainly wasn't a slave to sin, but the stuff I'd taken in through my life experiences had created soul junk. It had gone like this because I was living in this world.

Here I was, praying for the sick, and what I was doing was laying hands on them, reflecting back on my soul filtered through my body. It's body/soul, soul/body, and back out. Is anybody going to get healed that way? No.

CHAPTER 24

BRAZIL

The first impartation that changed the way I prayed for healing occurred when my wife and I were on a trip to Brazil through Global Awakening. I remember I was crying out to the Lord, frustrated again by fruitless praying through the soul. Brother Randy Clark was praying for the people to receive words of knowledge. He was imparting this gracing to the people on the trip, and I remember saying, "God, this is it. I need an encounter with You. I've got to know You! What do I have without You? There is nothing but You, God. If You don't show up, I've got absolutely nothing here. When I pray for the sick, nothing happens. When I don't get words for them, I don't understand why, Lord! But I know if You don't move in, I've got absolutely nothing. If it's not for Your Spirit moving, I've got nothing!"

Just then Brother Randy came to lay hands on me. I said to myself, "I'm not going to go down. I'm not going to go down!"

and Randy blew on me. "Receive!" *Puff.* "Receive!" *Puff.* "Receive!" *Puff.*

I did something you're not supposed to do. I grabbed the minister and didn't let him go. (I keep telling you stuff you're not supposed to do. Don't get any ideas, okay?)

I thought, "I'm not going down! I don't want to do the, 'Okay, I kind of feel God,' fall on the floor and then bounce right back up! It's got to be the real deal here." So I hunkered down. "You're not getting me down unless this is through God."

Brother Randy continued to blow on me. "Receive the Holy Spirit!" *Puff.* "Fire!" *Puff.* "More!" *Puff.*

It's funny what we do sometimes, isn't it? I'll look at videos of our meetings, watching what I do, and find myself thinking, "This is the strangest life! If people saw this, they'd think I was crazy."

After the fifth time Randy puffed on me, I don't remember anything; I was just out. Down for the count, and I felt this wave of peace come upon me like I've never felt before. I don't know for how long. A while. I guess I had to be carried around or something, because I ended up sorta, kinda waking up in a shopping mall. I was in the food court lying on the dirty ground. I'm serious here. I was sort of coming in and out, still enraptured in the Spirit. It took me a long time to come all the way to, but I remember telling the Lord, "No, I don't want to come back. I just want to stay in Your presence."

That encounter with God changed me. Shortly after, at a meeting back in America, many of us Brother Randy had imparted a word of knowledge anointing to were standing in a line. Suddenly, I felt this impression and said aloud, "I feel like God wants to heal this spot right here on someone's body." I touched the spot by my ankle.

A man in the front row started going, "Woo-hoo! Woo-hoo!"

Brother Randy asked, "Steve, what happened?"

It was the worship leader, Steve Swanson. He said, "When that guy up there touched that spot, I felt the pain leave my body. I had pain there." His right Achilles.

Can you imagine how I felt in that moment? All the disappointment over the years. I'd practically given up praying for people because it was too painful. This healing thing was too painful because "I ain't got it apparently." I had nothing. The people I prayed for just died. Hardly anybody ever got better. It was bad, and it had been tearing me up.

But in that moment when Steve got healed, all that pain got washed away. Years and years of frustration and disappointment just getting flushed. It was *cleansing* for me to see him get healed, because *I* had had that word of knowledge. After that, I started seeing people get healed when I prayed for them. That's when things began to open up for me.

I've said it before. People ask me all the time, "How do you deal with disappointment?"

I always respond, "You don't deal with disappointment. You're not meant to. You get victory. That's the only way you deal with disappointment."

I told you earlier my dad died of cancer in 2009, before I started walking in miracles, when I was still the man who was "least anointed." It was so terrible. But how do I get victory, now? I see people healed of cancer. That's my victory—I see people get healed of cancer and various diseases. That makes up for the pain and disappointment.

Whatever area of your life you seem to struggle with most, the area where you feel like a failure, that's probably the very area that

God wants you to walk in greatest victory. If you've got a history of bad, awful, broken relationships, the greatest blessing in your life is to have healthy, strong, good relationships. The enemy is just trying to attack that area more than any other.

That's what he attacked in my life more than anything. The greatest source of pain in my life was the healing ministry, and now that's the greatest source of blessing and pleasure. That's our God. That's the way He turns things around!

You want to know where you're probably the most gifted? Look at where the disappointment, the constant frustration, has been.

Maybe you've always struggled with money, money, money. Well, God has intended for you to have abundance, abundance, abundance.

It's time for victory. Take Him fast! That's how you deal with disappointment; you get the victory. It's only victory that washes away disappointment. "Dealing with disappointment" never works. That's just settling. Don't deal with disappointment—get the victory, and it will flush the disappointment out. That's accelerated healing!

CHAPTER 25

BRANHAM'S PULLS

I was always fascinated with William Branham, and as I understand it, Branham had three phases of ministry that were very, very powerful. He called them "pulls of the Spirit."

The first phase was a discernment of spirits gift in his hand. He would hold somebody's hand in his, and his hand would react—a kind of "buzzing" so to speak. If it was some kind of demonic disease, his hand would react a certain way, and he would know how to take authority over the affliction. In time, he learned how to understand the patterns he felt in his hand, and based on the way his hand reacted, he could tell what sort of disease he was dealing with. When that reaction in his hand went away, he knew the person was delivered and healed. Incredible gift, right?

That was the first pull of the spirit, and Dr. James has operated in this same kind of anointing for years. People say it's Branham's mantle; I don't know if I'd call it that honestly. Got to be careful not to say it's just "one person's mantle." James certainly doesn't claim that. Really, it was imparted to him through the ladies of the Golden Candlestick. Space doesn't permit me to go into that here. Read *The Dancing Hand of God* and the *Ladies of Gold* books if you're interested in learning more about this.

Anyway, the second pull of the Spirit was a visionary thing, and Branham would go into an open, outward vision, seeing very specific details of a person's life as a moving picture with his naked eyes. He'd be able to speak that into the person's life because all he was doing was describing what he was seeing. When he got the vision, he knew they were healed.

God only gave him these visions when it was *that* specific, and people got healed. It spilled over onto others in the congregation simply because that kind of "panoramic operation" (as it's been titled now) raises the level of faith in the room corporately.

James has operated in this panorama for years as well. Remember when I told you the story of the little girl who grew at the beginning of the book? That was panorama that he was operating in. Seeing that completely changed my life that day. I said, "I want to be with this guy!"

But I was crying out for the gift of faith—the third pull of the Spirit that Branham sadly never came into. God showed it to him, that he was supposed to step into it, but as we know, in his latter ministry Brother Branham unfortunately stepped off of some things doctrinally. I think most of us know his story, so I'm not going to go into details of that. We all know that the first part of his ministry was very pure, when he was surrounded by great advisors like Gordon Lindsay and had an accountability network in play.

Suffice to say, it is important for all of us to have people we trust—our spiritual fathers, as it were—who can help guide us and keep us strongly accountable to the unadulterated Word. Without it, we are all susceptible to getting a little weird in our theology. Enough on that.

Before that, God showed Brother Branham that the third pull of the Spirit was a gift of faith where he would speak things into being under the direction of the Spirit. It was a move of dynamic, creative miracles. Like when Jesus spoke to the fig tree in Mark 11.

> *"Have faith in God," Jesus answered. "Truly I tell you, if anyone says to this mountain, 'Go, throw yourself into the sea,' and does not doubt in their heart but believes that what they say will happen, it will be done for them. Therefore I tell you, whatever you ask for in prayer, believe that you have received it, and it will be yours. And when you stand praying, if you hold anything against anyone, forgive them, so that your Father in heaven may forgive you your sins"* (Mark 11:22-25 NIV).

This gift of faith was supposed to be like that—a true gift of the Father's faith imparted to the people. What a powerful impartation! I've cried out for this. "Gift of faith. Gift of faith."

The very first meeting I had with James Maloney, I discovered he'd never had anybody travel with him extensively before. He'd led teams for years, and there were seasons of impartation to congregations that the Spirit directed him to, but not a singular person consistently traveling with him. I was the first one.

Now, remember this is God, okay? He orchestrated this; otherwise, it wouldn't have worked for as long as it has. I'm not more "special" than any other member of the Body; I was put in a specific place by being open to this impartation of the Spirit, and there is a certain cost of willing to be poured out upon people in this way. Sacrifice of time spent away from my family, money for traveling expenditures, long nights of ministering until one in the morning, bone-tired overnight flights across the oceans, and much more. But I believe to a certain extent this can apply to all of us, even if we're not all traveling with James directly.

But we had this meeting with him, and I just asked, "So what can I do for you?" We started talking, and I remember saying, "I know what you're carrying. Branham died before the third pull of his ministry could happen. I believe in this day and age, the third pull is to come on the Body of Christ corporately." Now, it's not for *individuals*; it's for the Body of Christ. We are talking about a decrease of "self," so that there is an increase of Jesus corporately manifested through His entire Bride. That's why James' books deal so heavily with humility and character development. They are some of the two greatest (and, in many cases, most lacking) keys to accelerated healing. None of us have attained, but that doesn't negate the benchmark.

> *He must increase, but I must decrease* (John 3:30).

I got very bold with James. "I believe God's called you and me to release this." The third pull gift of faith.

He said, "That's right. You're the one. I want you to travel with me." That was many years ago. So I cried out because I knew he was carrying a gift of faith that the Body of Christ needed desperately.

CHAPTER 26

THE MAN WITH NO TONGUE

During one of these meetings, Dr. Maloney was operating in panoramic visions (read *The Panoramic Seer* if you don't understand this term), and the cloud of glory was so very thick it was almost tangibly visible. Now, James can stand up under that powerful cloud because he's the one ministering, but it's very hard for the person he's ministering to. They get caught up under that cloud of glory, and if a catcher or anybody else gets near....

Well, when I first started traveling with him, I saw people who would be like, "Oh, I want some of that!" because the glory's thick and tangible; they can feel it. "Yeah. Yeah. Gimme the glory!" And then they'd end up on the ground. I remember thinking, *You didn't have the fear of the Lord there, buddy. Gotta watch that.*

There were actually several instances when people would fall when they got near to that cloud. That may sound strange to you, but you know, this is a holy moment, right? And we'd better approach it with the right, reverential attitude of humility or get out of the way. While panorama *is* fun, it's also very holy. We can't mistreat it like some kind of Holy Ghost party, even if it is meant to be enjoyed.

I was kind of freaked out the first several times I was around this type of operation. I wanted everything, but I was cautious. I kept seeing too many people fall down, so I'd keep a little bit of distance, a place where I thought it was "safe" to stand and not get in the way. When James was ministering to a person, I would stand a bit farther away. I didn't want to get knocked down. Remember, I don't like getting knocked down.

But I was crying out for the gift of faith, and in this one meeting in Kansas I got the breakthrough. I was standing there, and Dr. James said, "John, step into the panorama."

Keep in mind, I'm already a little freaked out by the operation, and James is a big dude with a booming voice. By now we're really good friends, but early on I remember thinking he was a little scary. Imposing.

So he said, "Step into the panorama," and I wanted to be obedient, so I said, "Okay," and took a step about *that* close. A little baby step.

"John." James was just standing there. "Step into the panorama."

I said, "Okay," and took another little, tiny step.

Now he's starting to get mad at me, right? Because he's directing me, but it's right in the middle this ministry time with this lady, and I'm holding things up.

"John, step into the panorama *now*."

I'm thinking, *Oh God, oh God*, but I say, "Okay." Here I go. I'm expecting, you know, like I'm going to get blasted. *Please, God. Please, God.* Remember when Indiana Jones stepped into that tunnel and had to take a step of faith? It was kind of like that.

I remember thinking, *Okay, God, I just surrender this to You.*

James says, "John, receive the gift of faith."

And *bam*! James hits me right there in the chest, and I go down. It wasn't like the impartation from Brother Randy in Brazil, where I was out of it for hours. I wasn't really *out*. I just went down, and I thought, *Okay. I just believe I got it.* I say this to show it's not really the "feeling" that matters. It's received by faith.

It wasn't a radical "Ooh, I just felt this huge surge!" It wasn't like the first impartation. This time, I just said, "I got it." That was it. I didn't feel much. I mean, I *did* go down, but that's because he hit me!

But from that moment on, I could get as close to that panoramic cloud as I wanted, and the angel never pushed me down. It was like I was a part of the operation from that moment on.

Something had shifted. I noticed when I spoke something while ministering healing, and if the person believed the words that I was speaking, their healing manifested. That had never happened before until James said, "John, receive the gift of faith." *Bam*!

Hebrews 11:1 says faith is a substance. When you speak a word of faith, that substance is released. It's there. And when the person believes the word you've spoken, that substance materializes in the natural realm. This is the key to creative miracles.

Let me share a testimony with you. This is one example out of so many—it gets to the point where I can't keep track of how many creative miracles I've witnessed. That doesn't mean they ever get *commonplace*, for they're certainly not! But it does get to the point where the mind cannot recall all of the miracles that have taken place. God gets all the glory!

We were in a meeting in Oregon, and a man came up in the prayer line. Dr. James asked, "What would you like the Lord to do for you today?"

The man's reply was unintelligible, just garbled. "What?"

This man was pretty young, probably early twenties, and his wife was standing next to him. She said, "He was born without a tongue."

I remember thinking, *This is gonna be cool!* I'd seen so many creative miracles at this point, I just *expected* the guy would get a tongue. I looked into his mouth, and there was nothing there, not even a little stub. Absolutely nothing. I'm not sure how that affected his ability to eat. Seemed to me like you would need a tongue to eat, but somehow he did it. I couldn't understand him very well at all, but his wife sort of could. I remember he'd come with a lot of people.

So there's no tongue there at all. Dr. James goes into a kind of visionary thing, and he sees in the spirit the man's tongue being created, so he simply speaks what he's seeing the Father do. "I'm seeing you're getting a tongue." He says to me, "Stick your finger in his mouth."

"I'm not sticking my finger in his *mouth*."

So James says to the guy, "You stick your finger in your mouth, and tell me when you feel something there that wasn't there before."

The young man obeyed.

"Do you feel something?"

Now, remember when I told you about Naaman being instructed to dip seven times? Or it's like when Elijah sent his servant to go look for the rain, and he kept going back and forth saying, "There's nothing. There's nothing. There's nothing." Suddenly, on the seventh time he said, "Okay. There's something. I see a little cloud like a man's fist."

So at first, there's nothing in the man's mouth. Undeterred, James says, "Okay, do something, keep feeling for it. It's there."

I remember thinking, *Come on, when are you going to start feeling it? It's there.* I've reached the point in my walk with the Lord that if I say it, I know it's happening. Just believe it. As soon as you start to believe the words, it's going to materialize. Isn't it interesting how the Lord works? It takes an element of faith from both parties—the one praying and the one receiving.

All of a sudden, the guy gets a funny look on his face. Dr. James says, "You're feeling something that wasn't there before, aren't you?"

When he nodded his head, his tongue came out of his mouth on the spot. Pandemonium! People just freaked right on out. The man wasn't trying to be rude, but everyone wanted to see his new tongue, so he walked around with his tongue sticking out!

What was happening here? It's worth repeating Hebrews 11:1 tells us faith is a substance. When you speak a word of faith as led by the Spirit, the substance is released. When the person on the other end believes the words that you're speaking, exercising *their* faith, the substance materializes and the miracle occurs.

Let me also point out, when we're ministering out of faith through *love* the person is able to receive that word because it is represented in love. But if we're *only* operating in faith, without the love to focus the substance of that word, they may not believe you because you aren't ministering to them through love. In that case, the faith substance may not materialize. This is why faiths works through love (see Gal. 5:6). Love is vitally important in seeing faith materialize!

This is one of those absolutely undeniable miracles that just shifts everything, shifts the entire atmosphere in the place. Let me tell you, healing was pretty easy in that meeting after that happened! That's accelerated healing!

CHAPTER 27

DON'T LIVE A TWO-THIRDS LIFE

So what happens during impartation? Why did I go from praying for the sick and not seeing anybody get well to watching a tongue grow out of a guy's mouth? Randy Clark laid hands on me, and all of a sudden I started seeing miracles. Then James Maloney laid hands on me, and all a sudden something I didn't have before—faith—just sprung up. How is it possible to have any faith when you pray for people for decades and you don't see anybody get healed? That's like starting with pretty much *nothing*. What happened? Let me do a little visual.

I said before we have a body, we have a soul, and we have a spirit. The spirit contains *all* the power of God that we've been talking about in this book. Your spirit-man is perfected and lacks nothing. The Holy Spirit and our spirit working together—just powerfully powerful! Just wanting to be released, but we have this soul (remember, that's the mind, will, and emotions), and this soul is there from birth, shaped when we've lived our life a certain way.

Until we've engaged the life of the Spirit, our soul is like a type of shell around our spirit-man so that our spirit is suffocated by the experiences of this life.

When I prayed for the sick all those years, I was just taking in all those experiences from the outside, turning them inward, and then relaying them back out. So it's the body going into the soul, going back out the body. My mind, will, and emotions was the filter for the experiences my body had in the natural world. There's no spirit involved in any of this.

I was living a two-thirds life. This is similar to what Romans 8:2 calls the "law of sin and death." There isn't any "life" there. Second Corinthians 3:6 says it's the Spirit who gives life.

When a man or woman of God is operating in the power of the Spirit, there is an expression of a full life—the abundant life that Jesus talks about in John 10:10.

We have the phrase "Be around giant killers if you want to kill giants" for a reason. When you're around men and women who are moving in the power of the Spirit and they lay hands on you, your spirit-man expands to overcome your soul-man. The spirit gets a boost because of the Spirit operating out of their lives.

> *That He would grant you, according to the riches of His glory, to be strengthened with might through His Spirit in the inner man* (Ephesians 3:16).

If someone's operating in the glory of the Holy Spirit and they lay hands on you, that shell the soul-man had over your life cracks. The thing that was keeping you in bondage, that was keeping the miracles at bay, that was keeping the breakthroughs in your life from overtaking you—it shatters, and that life of the Spirit begins to seep through those cracks of the soul, opening bigger and bigger. And pretty soon those spiritual "rivers of living water"

(John 7:38)—that is the life of the Spirit—floods your soul with what is in the spirit.

Your soul doesn't have to work against you. When it's filled with that which is of the spirit, it works for you. Your spirit and soul and body are working together, and you hear from the Holy Spirit more clearly. You need your soul to hear from the Holy Spirit—that's why the Father gave you one—and then you need your body to release what the spirit-fed soul is saying.

It goes spirit, soul, and body, and we live from the inside out rather than the outside in. That's the beauty of being around men and women of God who are moving in the power of the Spirit. Your own spirit-man gets stirred up and activated. Instead of your soul squeezing the life out of your spirit and having control over your body, your spirit-man begins to exert its rightful place and dictate to your soul and body. It begins to subdue the garbage in the soul and body. That is a key to accelerated healing.

The spirit begins to drive out the junk of your soul and body that's been hindering and keeping your life held down in bondage for years. The cruddy experiences of life that have affected your soul and body are keeping your spirit from breaking through. Keeping your finances tied up, keeping your relationships messed up.

But pretty soon, the life of the Spirit begins to invade your soul. Then when you pray for the sick, you notice something happens because it's coming from your spirit, not your soul. It's originating in the spirit realm, not the soulish realm. Now, yes, it flows *out* through your soul and out through your body, but it's *originating* in your spirit-man. That's what Ephesians 3:16 is saying.

When the glory is imparted to your spirit-man, your soul goes, "Oh no! I'm losing hold." Good. That's when the life of the Spirit comes into play. That's what Romans 8 is all about! We're not supposed to be living according to the law of sin and death—we're supposed to be living according to the law of the life of the Spirit in Christ Jesus.

> *But you are not in the flesh but in the Spirit, if indeed the Spirit of God dwells in you. Now if anyone does not have the Spirit of Christ, he is not His. And if Christ is in you, the body is dead because of sin, but the Spirit is life because of righteousness* (Romans 8:9-10).

Those who are in the flesh (meaning soul and body) do not have the miraculous power to please God, but if God's Spirit is alive within them, they are not in the flesh but in the spirit. Romans 8:8-9

> *How God anointed Jesus of Nazareth with the Holy Spirit and with power, who went about doing good and healing all who were oppressed by the devil, for God was with Him* (Acts 10:38).

Now, if we are Christ's, the Spirit dwells within us, right? And if God anointed Jesus of Nazareth with the Spirit and power, then we, too, are anointed with the same Holy Spirit. Christ means "Anointed One"; ergo, Christ in you means the "Anointed One in you." Hence the reason we call ourselves Christians—"little anointed ones."

You are not *you*. When you got saved, you became Christ in you. I was John, but the moment I got born again and received the Holy Spirit, John singular died, and I became Christ in John. Christ in John is my new name. That's who I am. Before, I was "just John." But now I'm Christ in John. So, you are not you; you are Christ in you.

The Anointed One is in you, and He wants to be let out. The Anointed One reigns in your life; you're no longer in control because your life doesn't belong to you any longer. You gave it away to Him. It is He who wants to accelerate healing in your life!

CHAPTER 28

TWO-THIRDS IS ANTICHRIST

The title of this chapter may sound a little harsh, but that doesn't make it any less true. Christ the Anointed One goes around with you everywhere you go, and He wants to be poured out to everyone you meet. That is how the fame of Jesus is spread to the whole world—through you and me! Wherever you go, the Holy Spirit living inside you wants to be let out. He wants to accelerate His healing virtue in everyone you come in contact with.

> *And every spirit that does not confess that Jesus Christ has come in the flesh is not of God. And this is the spirit of the Antichrist, which you have heard was coming, and is now already in the world* (1 John 4:3).

Now an antichrist spirit is a spirit that denies *the* Spirit of Jesus as the Anointed One. It lives out of only two thirds of "life"—that is, the body and the soul, that which is shackled to the mundane, natural world. It denies the life of the Spirit, which was manifested in the incarnate Christ. All *antichrist* means is "anti-Anointed One." Anything that is anti-anointing, denying the Spirit, is antichrist. It really is that simple.

When someone is enslaved to living out of their body and soul only with no expression of the life-giving Spirit, that is antichrist. Many Christians aren't any different from people in the world because they are living out of their body and soul only. They have the Holy Spirit, true, but He's completely suffocated by an antichrist mentality, the two-thirds life.

They say, "Oh, I do what I *don't* want to do. That which I do I don't *want* to do. Oh no! What am I going to do? I keep doing this, when I wish I was like that." Sound familiar?

> *For what I am doing, I do not understand. For what I will to do, that I do not practice; but what I hate, that I do. If, then, I do what I will not to do, I agree with the law that it is good. But now, it is no longer I who do it, but sin that dwells in me. For I know that in me* (that is, in my flesh) *nothing good dwells; for to will is present with me, but how to perform what is good I do not find. For the good that I will to do, I do not do; but the evil I will not to do, that I practice. Now if I do what I will not to do, it is no longer I who do it, but sin that dwells in me* (Romans 7:15-20).

This is living a Romans 7 life, a two-thirds life. Paul goes on to say, "No! You live according to the law of the life of the Spirit, not the law of sin and death." Romans 8:2

You should be living a Romans 8 life. It's in the context of living a life lead by the Spirit that Romans 8:28 comes into play: "And we know that all things work together for good to those who love God, to those who are the called according to His purpose."

The Holy Spirit through your spirit-man should be reigning, not the other two thirds of your existence. Your soul and body are supposed to be cooperating with the Holy Spirit residing within your spirit. He is released through your spirit through the laying on of hands. After all, that's how people get healed, isn't it? Accelerated healing is brought to bear when we are in a place that our spirits rule over our souls and bodies. *Then* will all things work together for good.

Romans 8:14 says, "For as many as are led by the Spirit of God, these are sons of God." A mark of sonship is being led by the Spirit, not being led by your body and soul. Being led by your body and soul is living a two-thirds life, right?

Now, follow me here. The antichrist spirit is numbered 666 according to Revelation 13:18. And most of us know that 6 is the number for "man"—in triplicate (trinity) it's 666. So man pretending to be god, correct?

But I want you to think of that as a ratio now. What is two thirds? It's .666 repeating—it's two thirds, living a two-thirds life, denying the law of life of the Spirit. Living a two-thirds life is antichrist.

And it's alive in the Church today! Anyone in church who is not living their life submitted to the Holy Spirit—well, they might be saved, but the anointing is not being released. It is being stifled by the other two thirds. It's not being let out, so it's not making any difference. And whether it's intentional or not, that's still antichrist.

This is why believers need impartation, and that's why it was so big for Paul to lay hands on people and get them activated. Before I was activated, I was the least qualified person to talk about divine healing; now I'm going all over the world ministering healing. That's not me; that's God. That's an acceleration of the healing principle being multiplied through the laying on of hands. Believe me when I say, I'm not joking when I claim to have been the worst healing minister on the planet. Nobody was less anointed than me. I had the Holy Spirit, but He wasn't getting let out, and that does nobody any good.

When you receive impartation, there's a response to it—you've got cracks, and your soul is starting to lose control. That's what's happening when someone lays hands on you. Your soul is losing control, and you feel it as your spirit-man rises up and asserts authority, and it feels good! But then your soul tries to exert itself again like, "Yeah, you just felt that, but whatever."

If you go back to living and thinking the same way as before, and don't start thinking according to the mind of Christ—that is, the mind of the "Anointed One" who is in you—it is possible to re-stifle the Spirit. By embracing what happened, you can keep that flow going, and the crack just gets bigger and bigger. Pretty soon your soul is totally subdued by the spirit, which is where we all want to be. That's its rightful place, what the Lord always intended.

But if you don't do anything with it, going back to life as normal, thinking as normal, your soul will try to reassert dominance. "Okay. That was a good experience, but I'm going to shut this thing down now." If you let it, then you're back to where you started.

When the spirit-man gets that boost, that crack, I encourage you to go all out. Don't lose the acceleration! Start praying for the sick wherever you can—and yes, use wisdom, don't act like a lunatic assaulting every person you see in a wheelchair; but let's be honest, it's not hard to find sick people! If you're looking for opportunity, I guarantee the Lord will create those opportunities for you!

Start receiving love from your Father. The two-thirds life stifles that love because it stifles everything. "Oh, I can't hear my Father's voice. I can't feel His love." Most likely that's because of this thing here—the stifling of the spirit by the soul and body.

But when you receive impartation (when you receive out of the riches of His glory), that's when you are "strengthened in your inner man" by the Holy Spirit. The apostle Paul knew the value of this; he knew that's what people needed—the gift of faith, the third pull.

I believe every minister in any capacity *must* lay hands on the people. It is so vitally important, and sadly, there is a strong decrease in the importance of "laying on of hands" in modern charismatic circles. I don't mean to be critical, but so many ministers and pastors aren't consistently, regularly laying hands on people in the meetings.

But Hebrews 6 says it's a basic Christian foundation. Paul (or whoever authored Hebrews, if you don't think it was him) was saying, "Hey, get *this* before you move on to *that*." Laying on of hands is as basic as repentance from dead works and eternal judgment. In other words, this is where we *start*—we need to lay hands on folks! So how can we, as ministers, ignore this vital principle? It is one of the first keys to accelerated healing! Impartation through the laying on of hands.

To step into that, to speak things into being, and to live according to the law of the life of the Spirit—this is what made all the difference in the world to me. If I don't have the Spirit, I've got absolutely nothing. I had to come to that place, the conclusion that I didn't want to live out of my body and soul anymore. No more two-thirds life. I was so tired of failure!

CHAPTER 29

THE EXPOSURE OF THE SPIRIT

The healing ministry really reveals if you're living the life of the Spirit. Ministering to other people reveals that to you. And it can be an uncomfortable revelation. In the past, I have been guilty of thinking, "You know, I'm not that great of a Christian; but it's okay, because I'm doing better than a few other people. At least I'm not like *that* guy."

Sound familiar? I daresay I'm not the only Christian who's ever thought that. But then when you pray for the sick and nothing happens, you kind of realize you don't really have it, do you? It kind of exposes stuff, doesn't it? You think to yourself, "Scripture says *this*. But I'm *that*. So obviously I'm way, way off."

Bottom line, if people aren't regularly getting healed, somehow we're way off. That's not a condemnation, but it *is* a realistic observation. Scripture tells us, "These signs shall follow those who believe." Jesus commanded us, "Do this."

So if we're trying to do it and nothing's happening, something's wrong. The problem's not on His end. We just need to settle that here and now. The very definition of "God" is to be without flaw or limitation. The problem here is on our end, and the solution to the problem is living according to the Spirit. It has to be the Holy Spirit or nothing. There isn't really a middle ground if we want to see accelerated healing.

We've got to come to that place where if our spirits don't move us, then let's just forget it. That's why Moses in Exodus 33:15 said, "If Your Presence does not go with us, do not bring us up from here." God honored Moses for his decision to stick to his guns—"Either You're with us, or we're staying right here."

It's almost a sense of desperation. I got to that point. I said, "Forget this. If You're not in this, God, I ain't goin'. I ain't layin' hands on the sick if I don't have that life of the Spirit, because I know I've got absolutely nothing to offer anybody without You."

We truly have nothing to offer anybody without God's Spirit, because we're just as "off" as everybody else without His life flowing through us. But, thankfully, we *do* have God's Spirit residing within us—we just have to let Him out; and once you get a taste of the Holy Spirit and you get that life flooding into your soul, you begin to guard it much more closely.

You start watching what you say, what you think, how you act; you learn not to hold things against people, because you don't want *anything* to clog up that flood. You begin to value Him so much more once you've tasted of Him. Then you watch what movies you see, what music you listen to, what books you read. You become much more sensitive what you permit to enter your mind, because you don't want to grieve Him. You want to hear the still, small voice and let nothing clutter it.

The life of the Spirit begins to get activated in you. You see the difference it's making in the lives all around you because you're bringing Kingdom reality with you wherever you go, whereas before you weren't bringing anything but words. I reached the point where I couldn't live with just words anymore.

Paul said, "And my speech and my preaching were not with persuasive words of human wisdom, but in demonstration of the Spirit and of power, that your faith should not be in the wisdom of men but in the power of God" (1 Cor. 2:4-5). When a person lacks anointing they tend to rely on psychology for explanations and solutions.

If you can *talk* somebody into the Kingdom, they can be talked out of the Kingdom just as easily, right? But if you demonstrate the love of God and the power of God hits them, it's much more difficult for them to deny that.

People try to tell my wife, "Well, you're just overplaying what happened to you." She says, "Hey, talk to the knee! The knee's healed. What else can I say?" It's like, I was blind, now I see. She just tells people, "I don't know what you're arguing about. You see this? I couldn't do that before, so you can choose to believe it or not, but it's my reality."

Yes, some people think she's nuts—you're not going to get 100 percent response. But a lot of people receive, and it's not up to you, anyway, if they accept the truth. You're simply there to present the reality of a supernatural God.

See, for those of you who've received a healing from the Lord before, even if you're not a super evangelist yet, you've got your testimony; and in many cases, that's enough. The reason why your testimony is so powerful is because it is filled with faith—you know it to be true, so it is loaded with the substance of faith. My wife loves God and loves people and —she just shares her testimony wherever she goes. If they'll receive that, they'll enter the Kingdom. Works for us.

You say, "Hey, this is what God did in my life," and then they see the reality of it, whether they choose to accept it or not. You're not just speaking words and rhetoric at that point, some clever phrase you learned out of a book. You're offering tangible proof that God's power touched you. Testimonies are important!

I used to try to minister to people without living in the Spirit, and when my life was a mess the people could see it. "What have you got to offer me? You're hardly better off!" There is a longing in every person's heart for God, whether people choose to pursue that or not. And if that longing is not satisfied in your own life, other people instinctually will sense it—because they have the same longing!

Before, I'd try to tell people about Jesus, and they'd be like, "Yeah, okay, thanks. Appreciate it. Thanks a lot. Well, I'll see you. Yeah, no, that was good. Bye now." In their minds, I know they were thinking, "That guy's just as goofed up as me, and I know it. What's his religion done for him?" That's the sad reality of it.

But when you're bringing something to them that's different and you're moving in the boldness and the power of the Spirit and people are getting healed, they can try to deny it, but ultimately it's futile. And the majority of people don't deny it. I have found that, on the whole, most people are open to seeing something from God. Sure, there's a "spirit of stupid" on some people, as Dr. Maloney says; they wouldn't receive a miracle if Jesus stood in front of them! But *most* folks are desperate to see some kind of supernatural reality in this life.

Most people engage, and they're like, "Wow, I just got healed! Surely God is in this place." We need more demonstration of the

Kingdom in our daily lives and ministry opportunities. We need accelerated healing!

Paul figured this out. "I didn't talk with human words of wisdom. I didn't come to you with eloquence of speech. I'm not the best speaker out there. Whatever. I showed you the power of God." You know, we always think of Paul as being this huge, spiritual giant with a booming, commanding voice: "Get saved!" And the people shriek, "Ah! He's freaking me out. I'd better get saved!"

We know on at least one occasion someone fell asleep as Paul preached. But Paul demonstrated the power of the Spirit, the "normal" of living a Kingdom life. Just like the guy in Lystra. He heard Paul preach, but it was more than just words. He connected with God, Paul saw it, and shouted, "Stand up! Get on your feet!" In the Kingdom life, the words you speak have anointing on them. It is that anointing that breaks the yoke, not just what you say. We release that anointing through our words, and that is what exposes the Spirit to the world around us.

CHAPTER 30

FACING REJECTION

I remember there was this lady in Redding, California; she was probably in her 90s, and she was still driving. I watched her park and move very slowly to get her walker out of the car. I was moved with compassion as I watched her struggle, so I went over to see if I could help her. But by the time I got there, she was already shuffling off with the walker.

Feeling this rush of sympathy for her, I blurted out, "Is there something I can pray with you for?"

The old woman looked at me for a second, then said, "I don't want prayer. Get out of my way!"

Suddenly, she was moving away from me much faster than she was before. Granny was hotfooting it out of there! I was floored. I wouldn't have expected that from a ninety-year-old woman. Would you?

So do you want to hear what happened next? Am I building the suspense? You want to know?

Absolutely nothing. That was the end of the story. She shuffled off, leaving me standing there shocked. I never saw her again.

Why would I tell you stories like that? If ministers come and all we do is give you the greatest hits, you're going to go out there and think something is wrong when things don't go right. When somebody rejects you, when somebody yells at you, you're going to think, "Oh. I must not be like that minister so-and-so. It always works for them!"

I don't want to present you with something false, something that is not what it is really out there in the world. For every person who comes to the Lord, probably another person doesn't. So terribly sad, but nonetheless true. Does it sound callous to say that's okay? We can't *force* people to receive from God.

I look at Jesus, and the Gospels don't mix it up. They don't say that everywhere Jesus went, it was water into wine and fragrant roses blooming in the warm sunshine. He went to Nazareth, and they wanted to throw Him off a cliff! That's a bad ministry day, wouldn't you say? I don't think I've had a ministry day quite *that* bad.

Think about that. Here you're preaching, the presence of God is all over you in power, and the next thing you hear is, "That dude's a phony. Grab him! Let's throw him off the cliff!" Yikes, talk about disheartening.

Jesus had some really, really bad ministry days. If we're looking at the results more than we're looking at the heart, if we're not living out of the voice of God, being obedient to His promptings, then we can get tired of the rejection. That's when we burn out. That's when we lose our joy. That's when we get our heart in the wrong place.

You could be led by God to speak to a person, and God fully knows they're going to reject what you say, but He'll still lead you to that person anyway. It's not up to you if they're open to it or not. Your job is to present the truth, to establish an opportunity for an encounter.

Thing is, you might be tempted to think, "I've missed God here. Obviously I didn't hear Him right, because they would've received me if it had truly been inspired by Him."

Not necessarily. Was Jesus being disobedient? Did He miss God when He went to Nazareth and made those declarations and proclamations? Was He mishearing the Father? Obviously, the answer is no. Well, then why was the result so bad?

Why would God lead you to a setup only to face rejection? The answer is God is a just God, He gives people every opportunity. He knows what He's doing. So maybe the person rejects you initially, and then maybe later on, they think about it. Maybe they turn around later on.

We don't always know the end result, but all I know is that God is completely good and completely just. We simply need to be open to Him using us in any way He possibly desires. We leave the results up to Him.

The point of all this is, don't allow discouragement to scare you off or burn you out. Don't think you've missed Him, and don't let it affect your heart. Jesus could've easily let that moment dishearten Him. Then He would have missed out on what happened next—the breakthrough, the amazing healings and miracles in Capernaum. Jesus never thought that He missed God—He never questioned who He was.

I'm sure every minister out there could give you just as many rejection stories as they could victory stories. I'd virtually guarantee it. And while we shouldn't be fatalistic or critical, if you know ahead of time that you might face rejection, then it doesn't freak you out quite as much. Now, I don't *like* it, just to be straight with you. I'd rather have everybody get saved, everybody get healed, everybody get delivered. I don't want to see anybody miss out, and neither does God. God wants to see everybody, without exception, meet Him and be changed in all facets of their lives. He wants everybody to enter in and experience Him firsthand.

But we need to recognize it might not be their moment just yet, even if God created that moment especially for them. They might need more time, and hopefully they will get it. God is gracious and longsuffering, and regardless of His intentions He will never violate a person's will. If they don't want to meet with Him, they don't have to—to their loss—and we all hope and pray it's not their *permanent* loss; but it happens, as sad as that is! God never forces Himself upon anyone. We need to understand that principle and be okay with it. Remember, it's Christ *in you*, not *you*. Never lose your joy.

CHAPTER 31

STRENGTHEN THE INNER MAN

My wife, Janet, has always had a beautiful voice; she's an operatic singer and former University Professor. Her vocal talent was always there, but it wasn't always anointed. It was just an amazing voice. But after Randy Clark laid hands on her, we noticed that whenever she sang, the presence of God would come. Her singing was suddenly anointed, and the glory would fall so thick, people would get healed just while she was singing. How cool is that?

When you live the life of the Spirit, there's anointing on every word you utter in the name of the Lord. When you receive impartation, when you begin to live according to the law of the life of the Spirit in Christ Jesus, you're never the same; you're changed in a moment. That's all it takes; you really *can* be changed in a moment. My wife has never been the same. I've never been the same since those two impartation encounters. That victory of the spirit man crushes every disappointment in your life, and from that moment forward you really are a different person.

People will see the Spirit's authority upon your words; they'll notice there's a difference. It's amazing how they can pick up on the changes in your life. You could say the exact same words when you were living out of your body and soul, and the people would be like, "Okay, that's cool. See ya." But if those same words come from the energized spirit-man out of an expression of godly love for the person, many people will react completely differently. I know this firsthand; I've seen it work time and again.

The Holy Spirit makes all the difference in the world. Treasure Him, honor Him, glorify Him. He increases the flow of life from that stance. You know, when we say, "Holy Spirit, come!" we're not just saying, "Come down out of heaven." That's already been done, right? You have the Holy Spirit inside you already.

What you're actually saying is, "Holy Spirit, come out of my spirit, into my soul, and flow out of my body. Strengthen my spirit-man, enter my soulish life, and transform it, so I can express it to others."

The life of the Spirit makes the most difference by entering into our souls, changing the mind, will, and emotions to reflect the truth of the spiritual Kingdom inside us. It changes our messed up thinking that isn't in line with Kingdom reality. When we experience Him in our souls, we become sensitized to detecting Him in our physical bodies. I believe the Lord intends for all of us to *feel* Him in our natural five senses. It's from there that we can release the power of the Kingdom in other people's lives. We'll start getting words, seeing pictures, even our bodies will cooperate with the Spirit. All things working together for good. Then your soul's not working against you. Your body's not working against you. You're coming into Kingdom alignment.

I know people who get healed because they get activated in the spirit-man, and pretty soon all kinds of fun stuff starts happening.

I've seen them start losing excess weight! Their mortal bodies are transformed to reflect the life of the Spirit, and they're not doing anything different calorie-wise.

And, sure, I know all our bodies are wearing away. I understand that. That's going to happen to us eventually, because the Scripture says we're going to get new bodies. But in the meantime, in order to maximize our time on this planet, to fulfill what God has called each of us to accomplish, we need to live in the healthiest bodies we can.

I'm sure my wife won't mind me sharing this, because it's such an awesome testimony. She used to be overweight, and one day she received prayer from a group of people. As weird as it sounds, she had an inner vision of a straw stuck into her skull, down into her body, and something was sucked out.

Now, I don't have a chapter and verse for this kind of experience; I'm just sharing what she saw in her spirit. Usually I try to find an accompanying scripture, but in this instance you'll just have to take our word for it.

She didn't do anything different. She didn't eat differently at all, but after these people prayed, she had this "straw vision" and asked the Holy Spirit, "What was that?" He replied, "I'm delivering you of a poverty spirit that was causing your body to hoard food."

I had never heard of such a thing before. But from that moment on, she started losing weight. She got thinner without changing her diet in the slightest. It was amazing to watch. She'd struggled with this her whole life, but the life of the Spirit began to transform her from the inside out. She looks completely different now.

We've been married over twenty years, and she's more beautiful than ever before. There's a reason why I'm always smiling! God is so good.

There's almost a spiritual "buffness" that comes from the strengthening of your inner-man by the Holy Spirit. When you feel that strengthening come on you, it's like the Holy Spirit's flexing His muscles through you. I'm not talking about confidence in the flesh here; that's why Paul buffeted his body into submission to his spirit (see 1 Cor. 9:27). It's the confidence of God in us. I think it's time we start having some spiritual swagger.

As we wind this book down, I just want to say thank You, Lord, that the soulish hold that's been stifling the life of Your Spirit within us is being broken! I pray out of the riches of Your glory, Father, that we may all be strengthened with mighty power in the inner-man by the Holy Spirit. Crack the shell around our souls, Lord, and flood out all the garbage with the goodness of Your liquid love!

Dear readers, let me leave you with this—all of us need to seize the moment, to take it fast. Remember, faith is not passive; it is an action, the very bedrock of accelerated healing. We do the small possible; He does the absolute impossible. "By faith the walls of Jericho fell down after they were encircled for seven days" (Heb. 11:30). There is an action involved. "By faith Abel offered to God a more excellent sacrifice" (Heb. 11:4). He brought an offering, and so should we.

"And whoever falls on this stone will be broken; but on whomever it falls, it will grind him to powder" (Matt. 21:44). Let's be broken, not ground to powder—fall on the Rock and break. And for those of you reading this who have already been "cracked" in their spirits, let's just stand in faith together that those cracks get even wider! More of the Spirit's life flooding out of you than ever before! Amen!

ABOUT JOHN DAVID PROODIAN

Dr. John Proodian is a former university professor and his passion is to see the love of Jesus manifest in the lives of others through healing, signs, and wonders. John's passion is to activate the Word, while proclaiming the Word, enabling people to step into the moment and encounter the healing power of Jesus.

John was a huge failure in the healing ministry for years and now is so grateful to see the lame walk, the blind see, and many other miracles by the power and love of God. If such a colossal failure in the healing ministry can lay hands on the sick and see them recover (Mark 16) than anyone can. John's passion is to equip the saints for the work of the ministry.

John and his wife Dr. Janet Proodian who is a professional singer, former university professor, and prophetic minister, are graduates of Randy Clark's Global School of Ministry and are both ordained by Dr. James Maloney. John is the author of *Accelerated Healing* and is honored to be on staff as a board member and executive associate evangelist with Dove on the Rise International.

His education in the Spirit has come from years of ministering side-by-side with his friend, mentor, and spiritual father Dr. James Maloney. Together they have travelled the globe, proclaiming and releasing the Kingdom of God in signs, wonders, creative miracles, prophetic ministry, and healing.